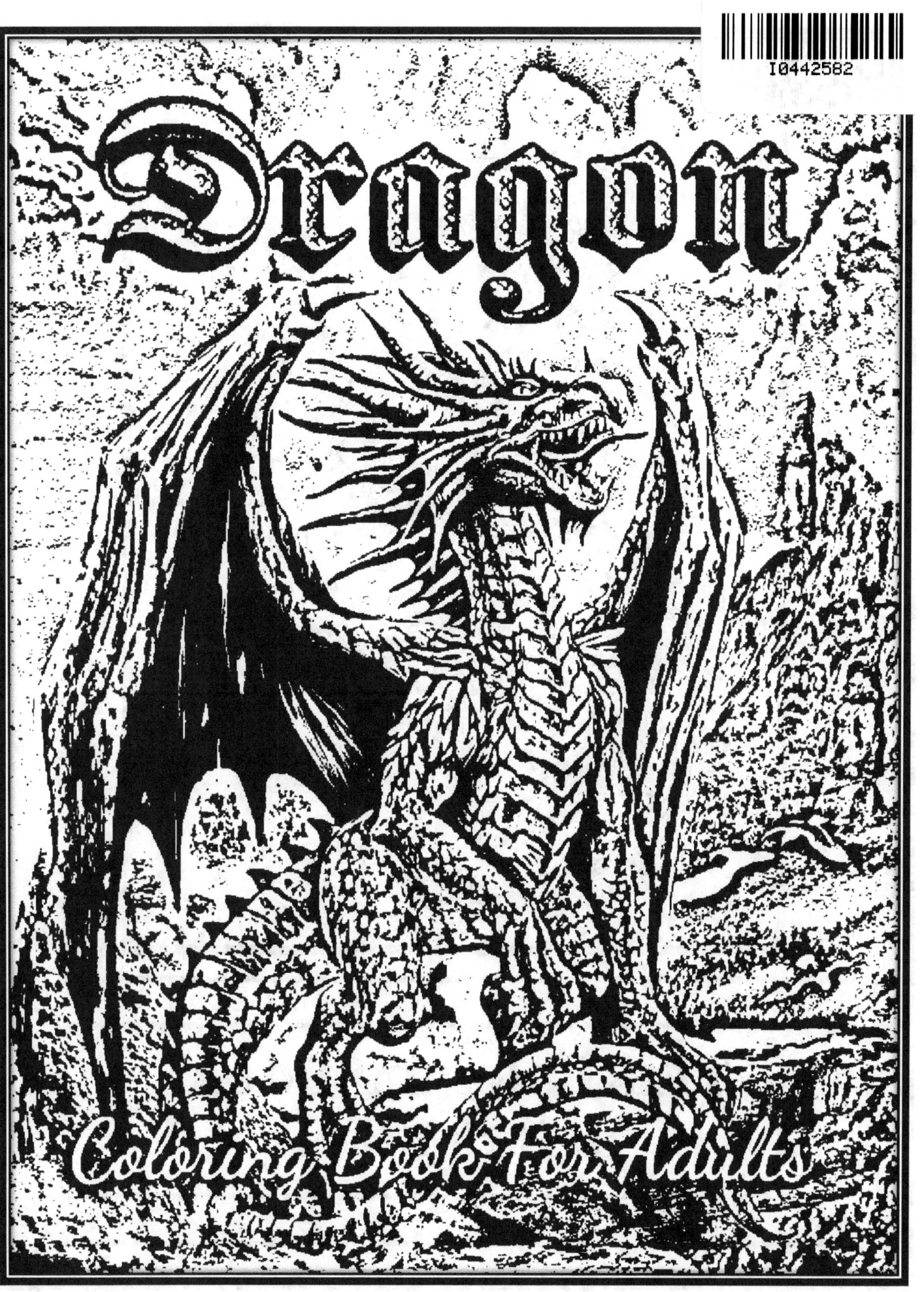

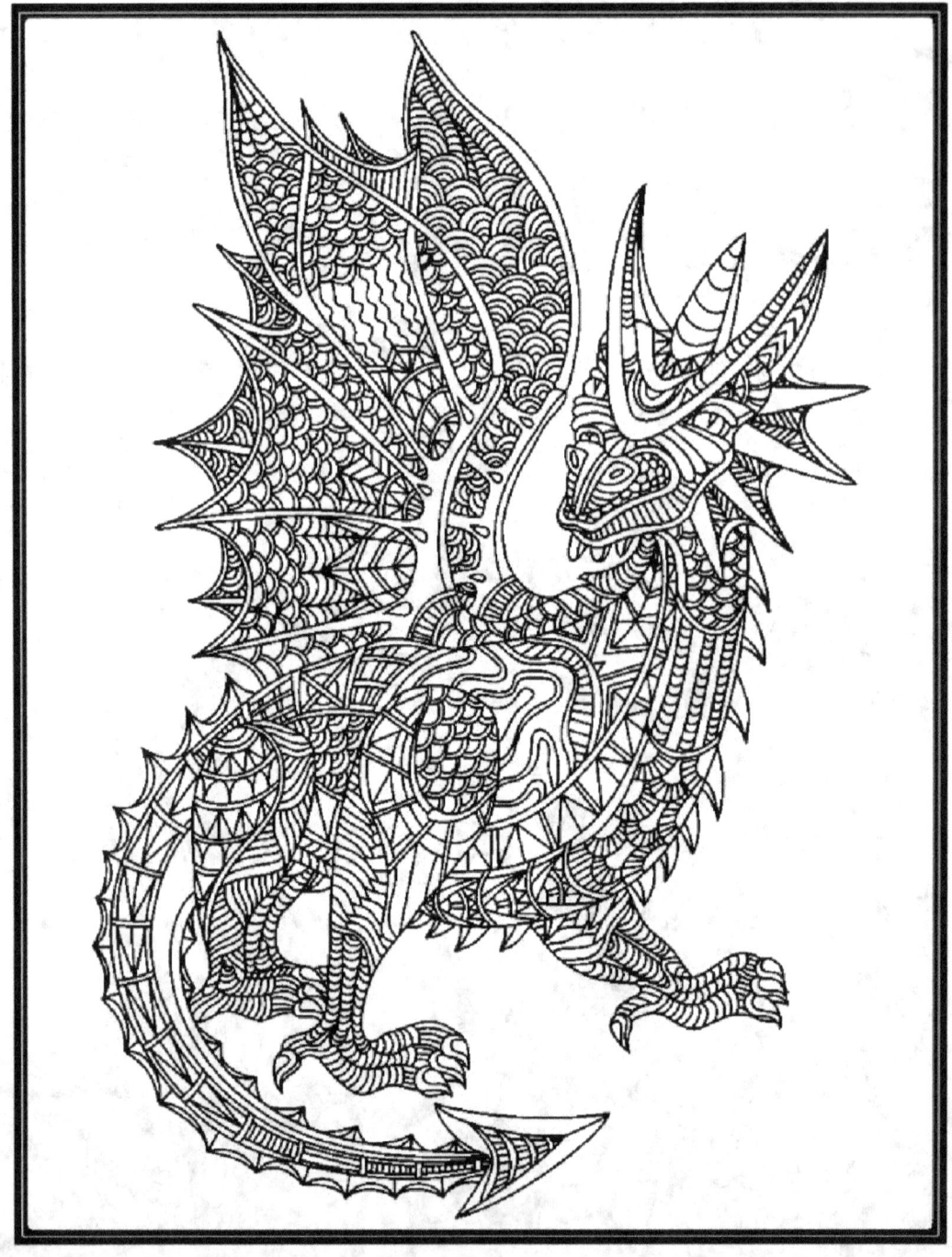

This Coloring Book Belongs To:

*Thanks for choosing this book. It's great that you like Coloring book.

*This book provides huge stress relieving Designs for Relaxation ! It will also help you to learn about the use of color.

* You will have the opportunity to develop your motor skills through coloring. We've included many unique and beautifully designed pages here that will keep you entertained.

Color Test Page

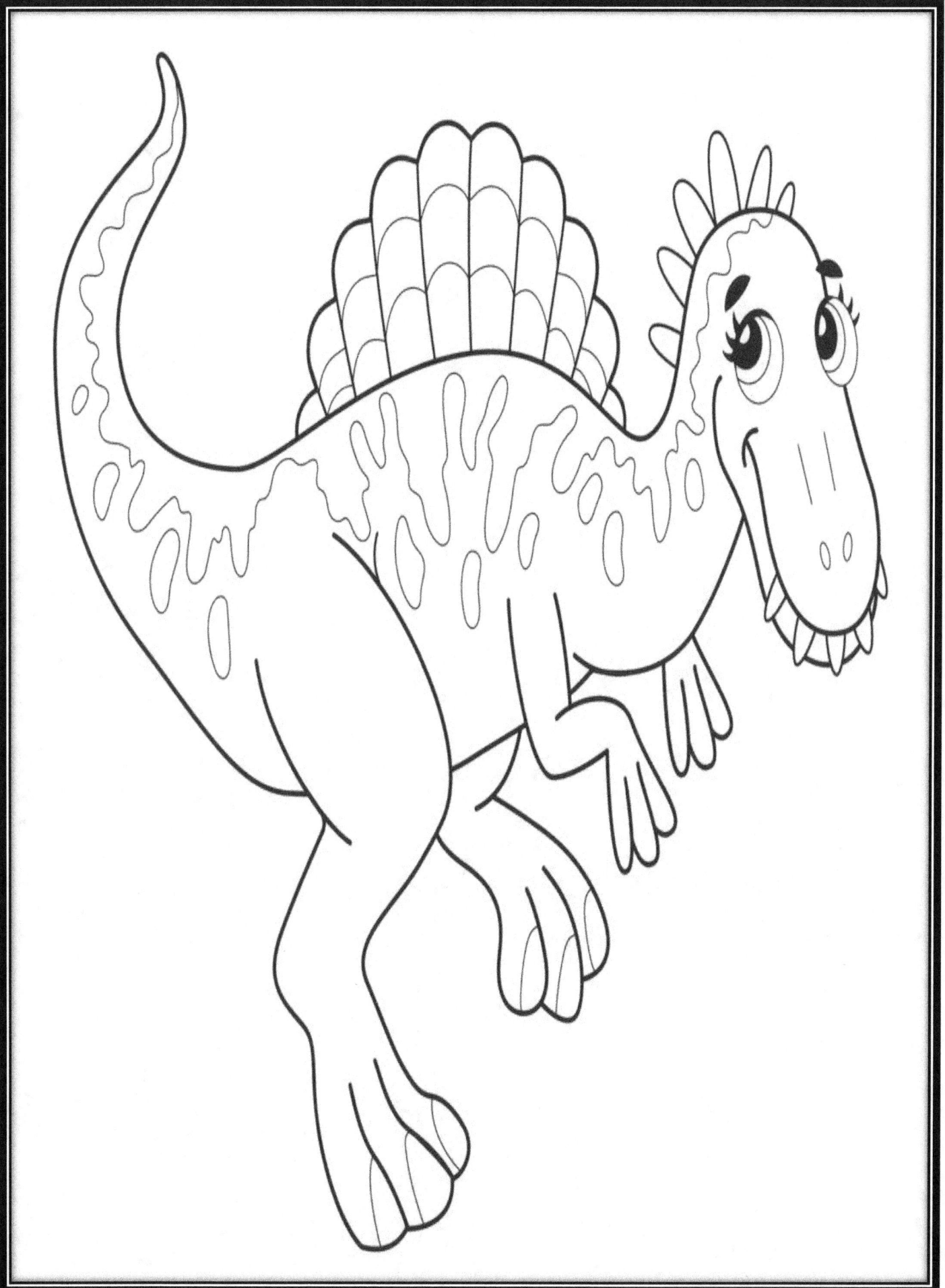

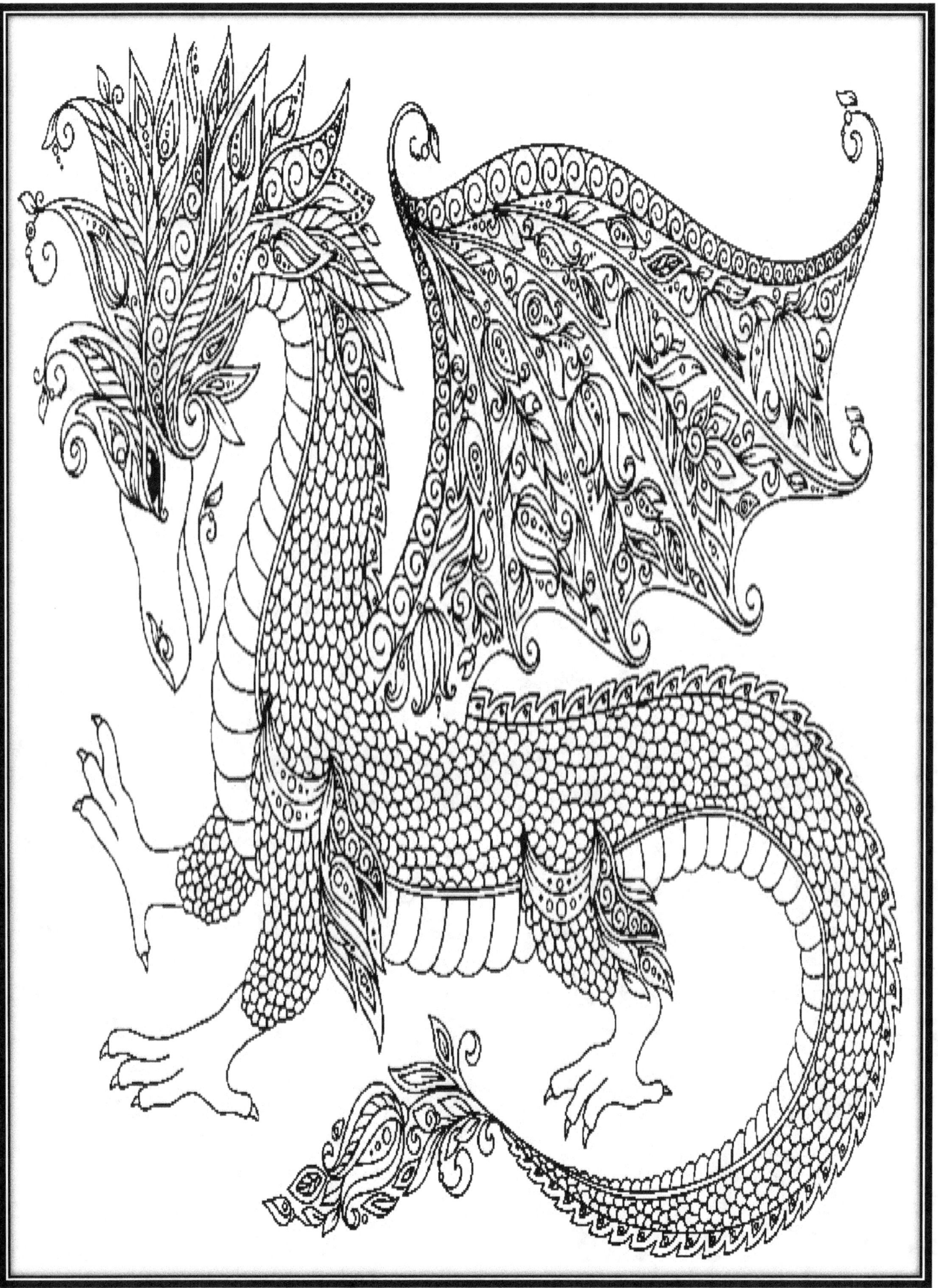

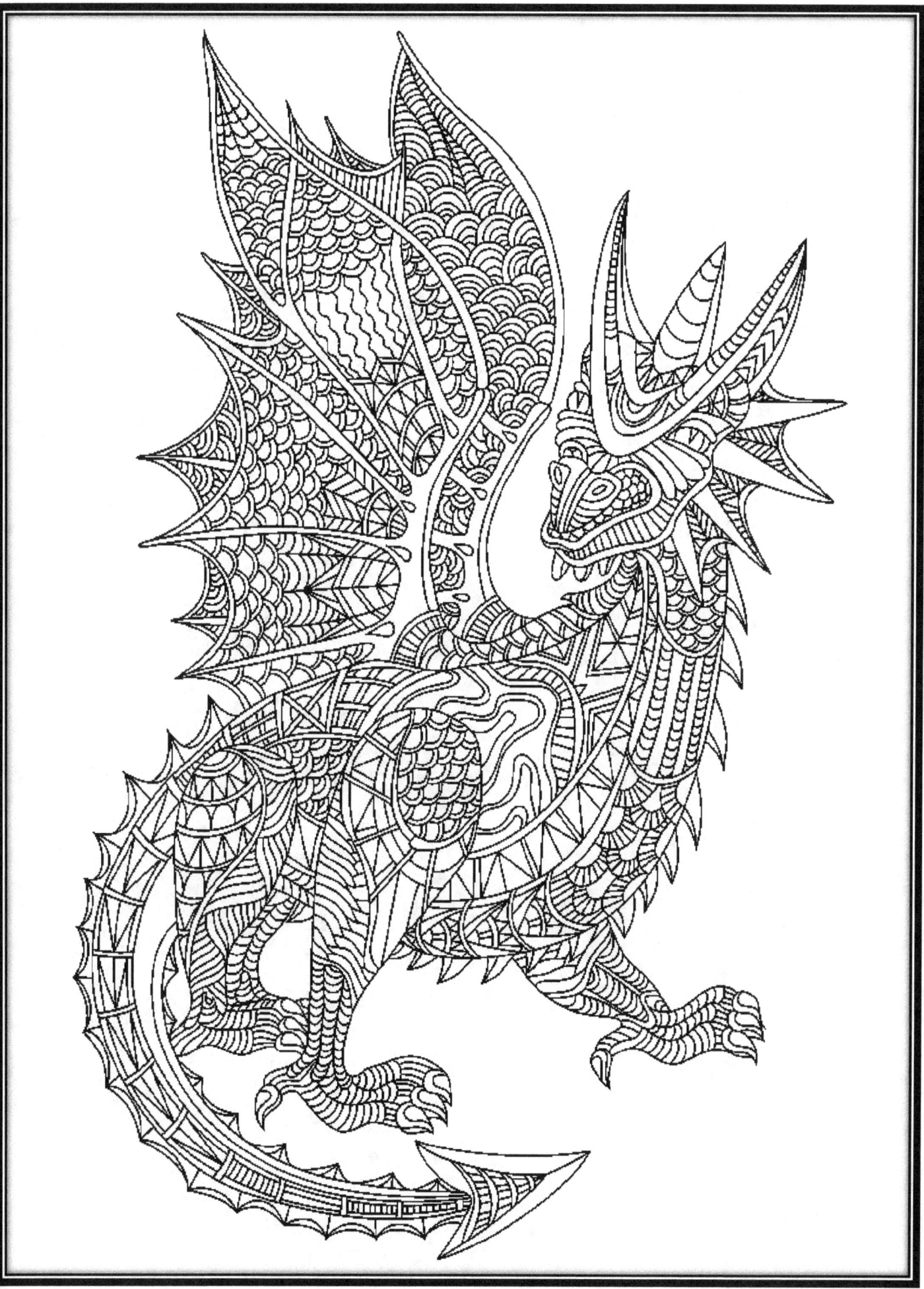

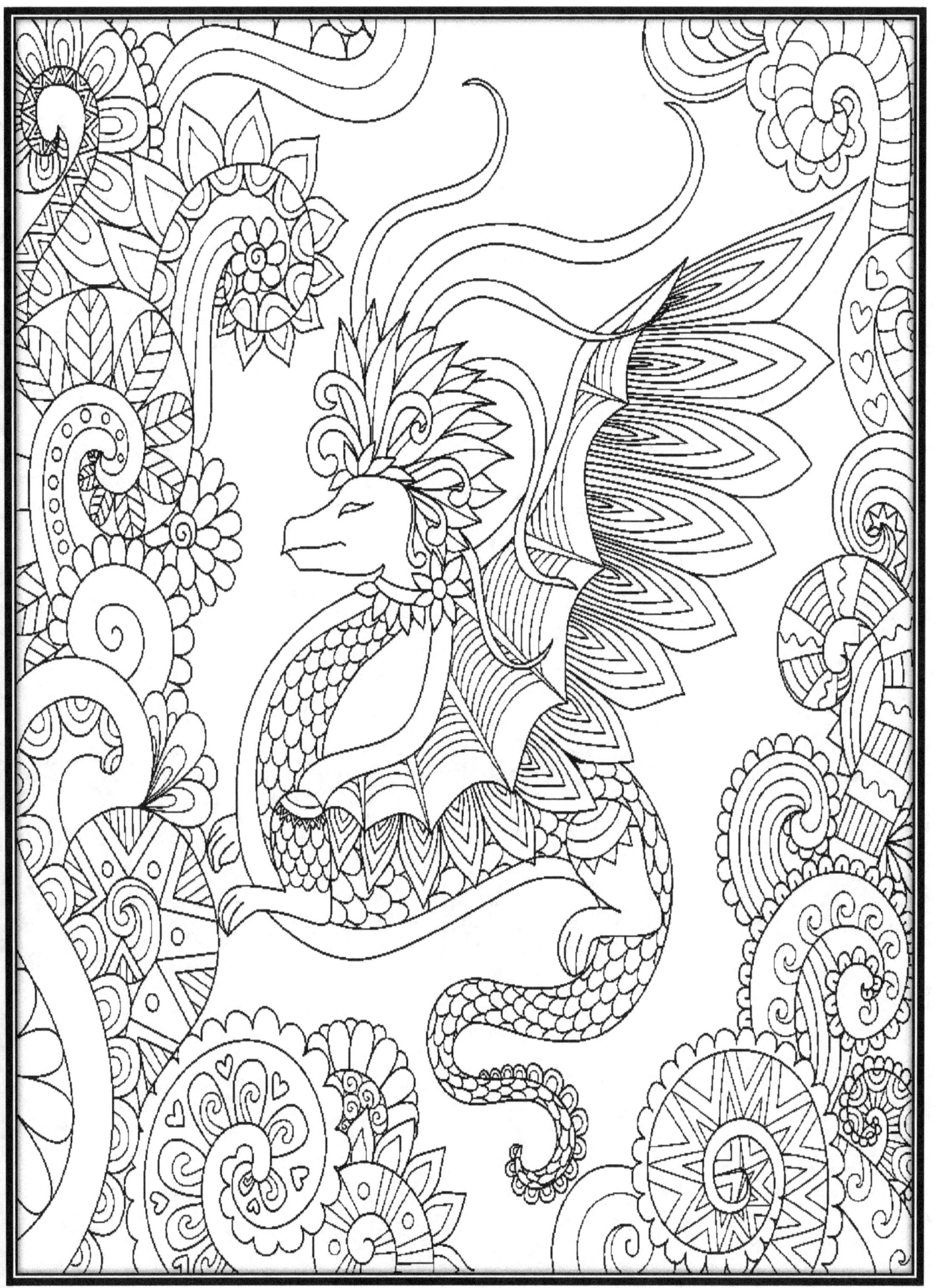

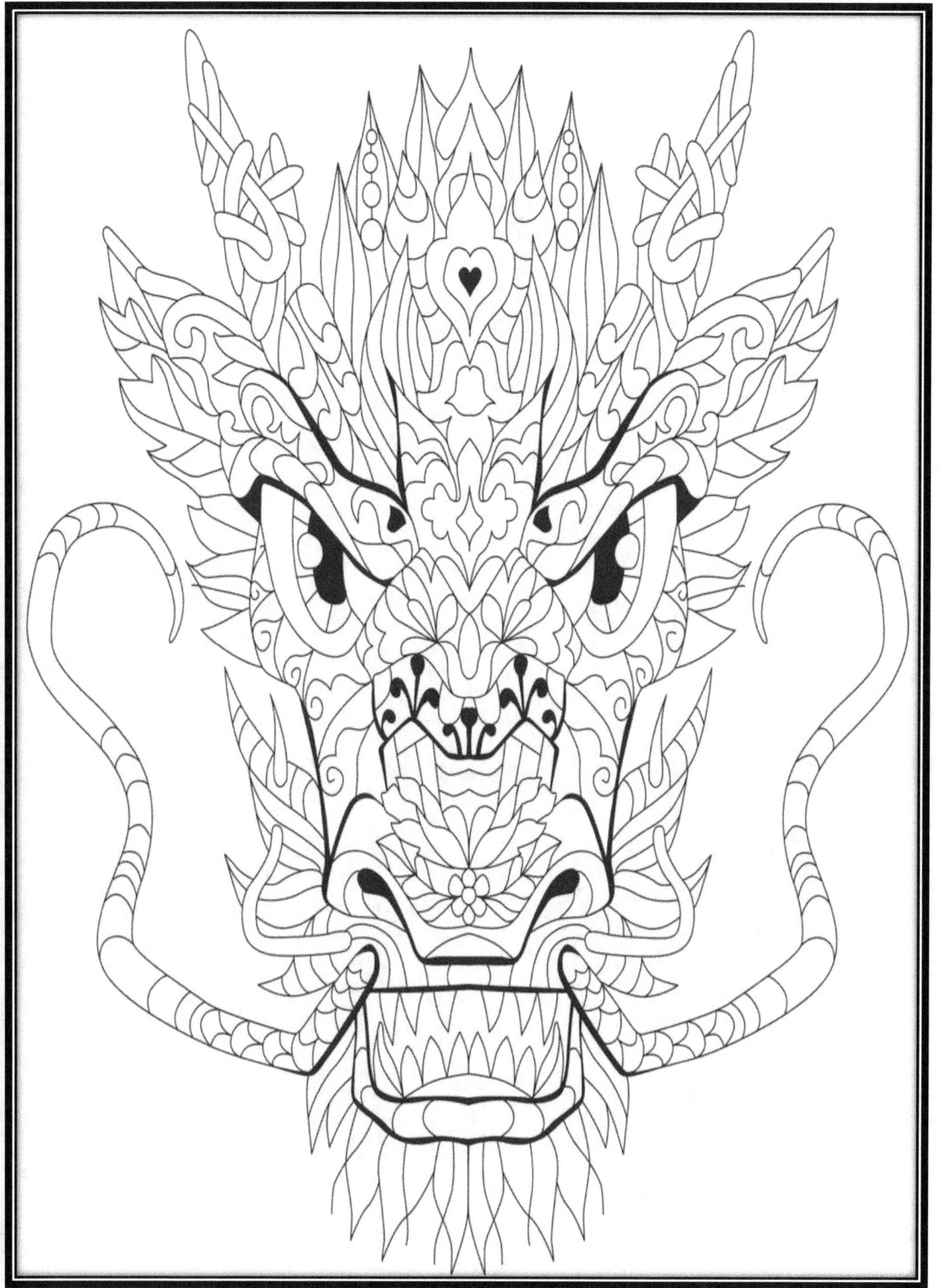

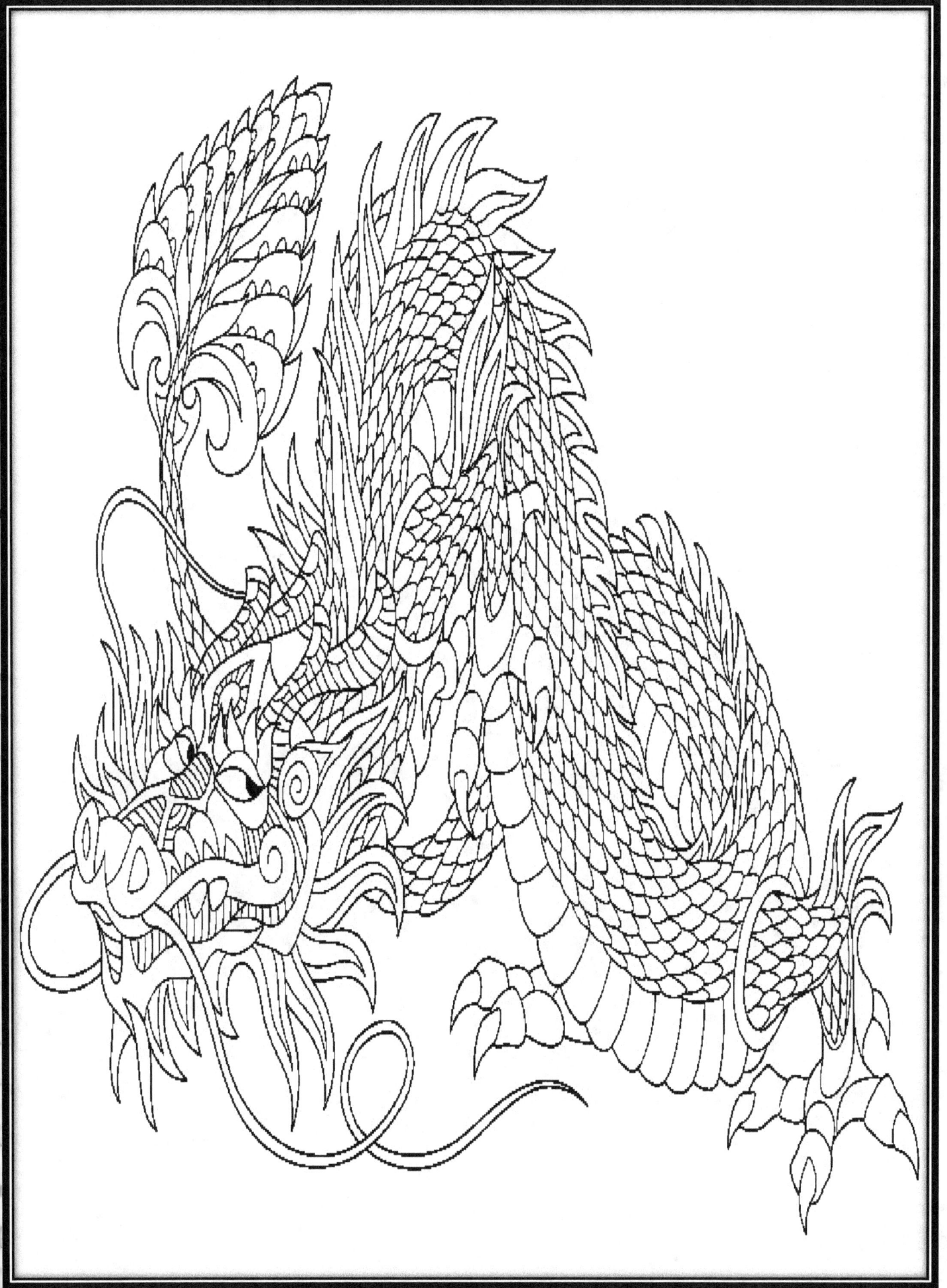

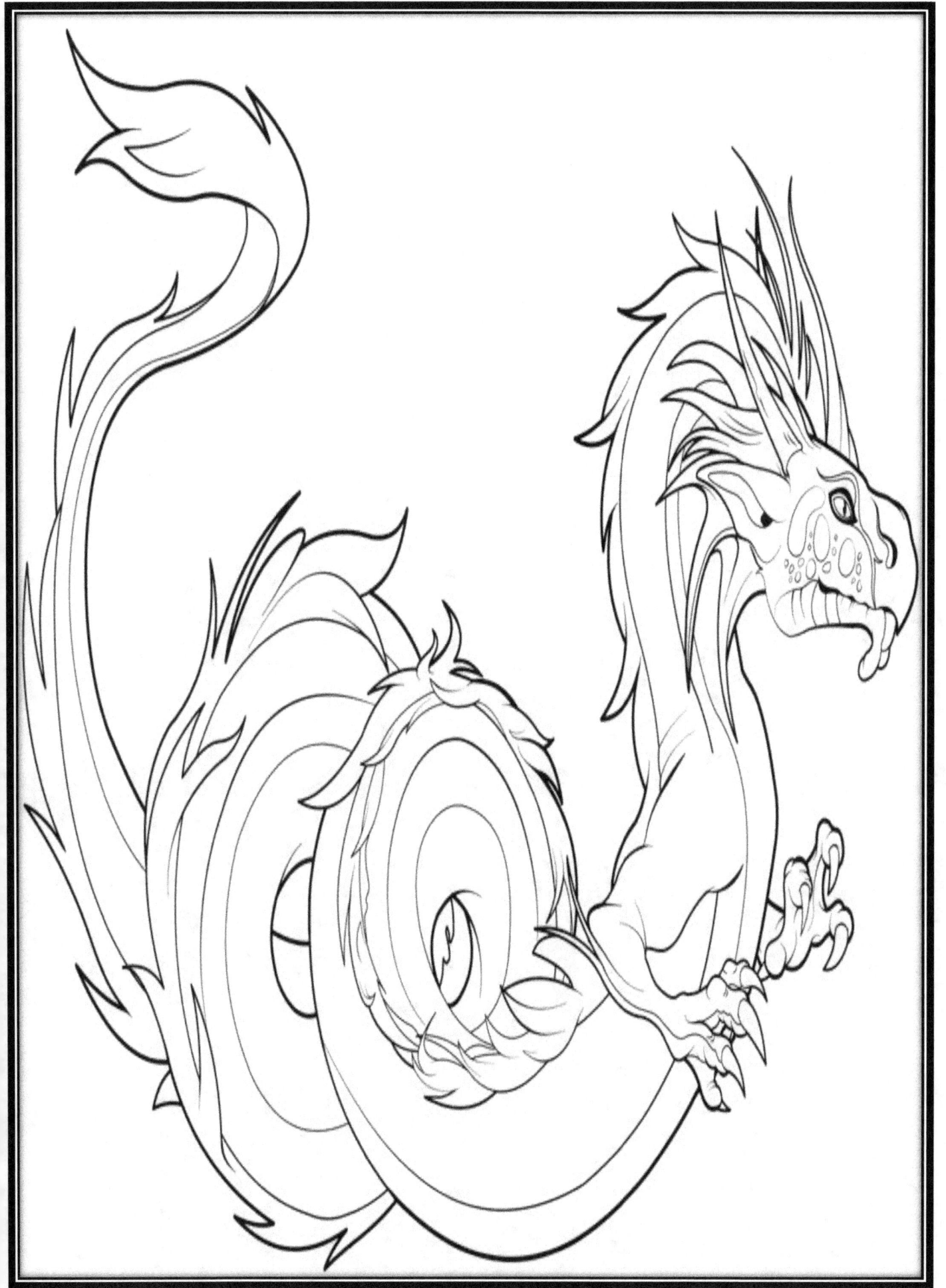

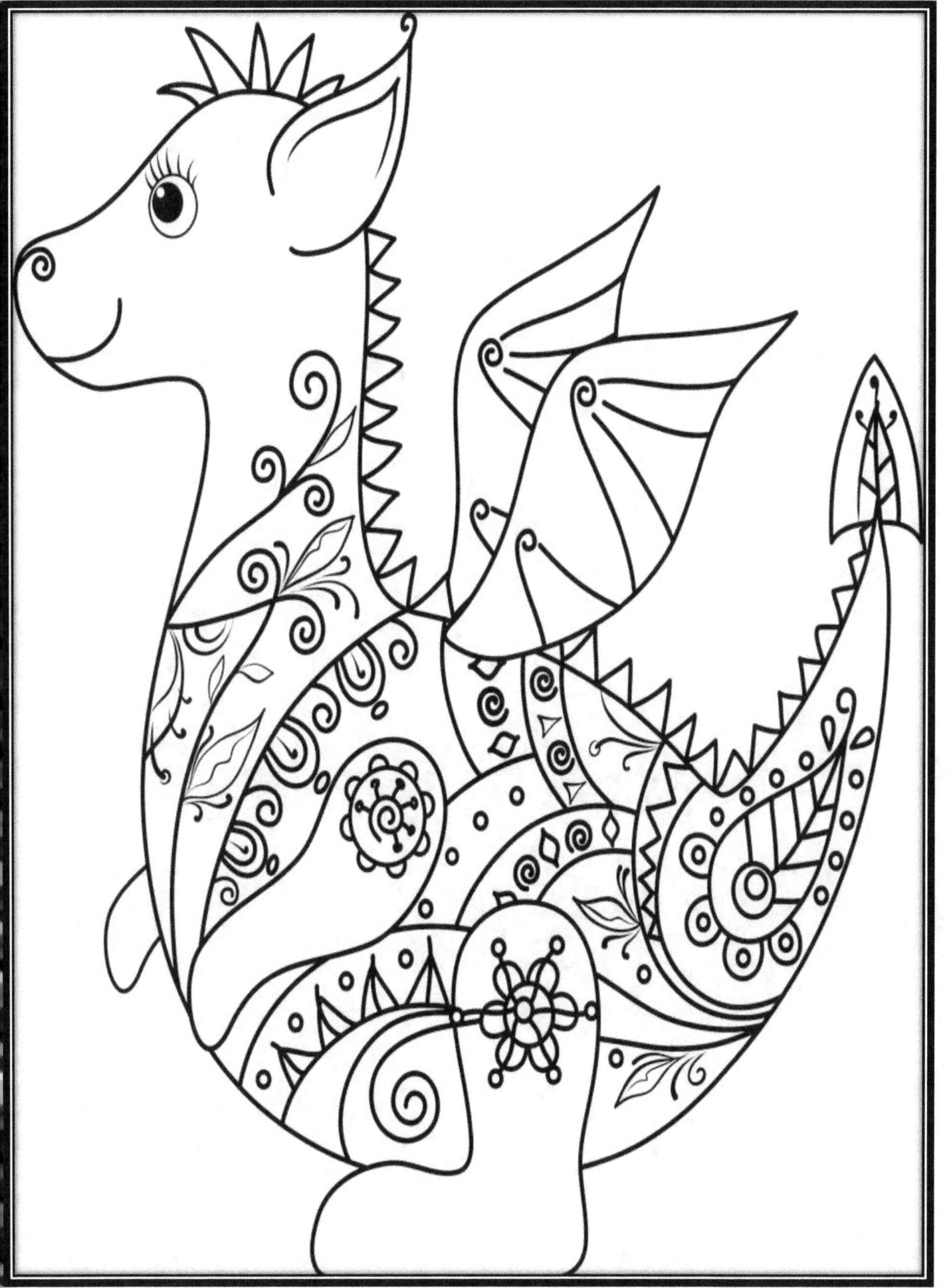

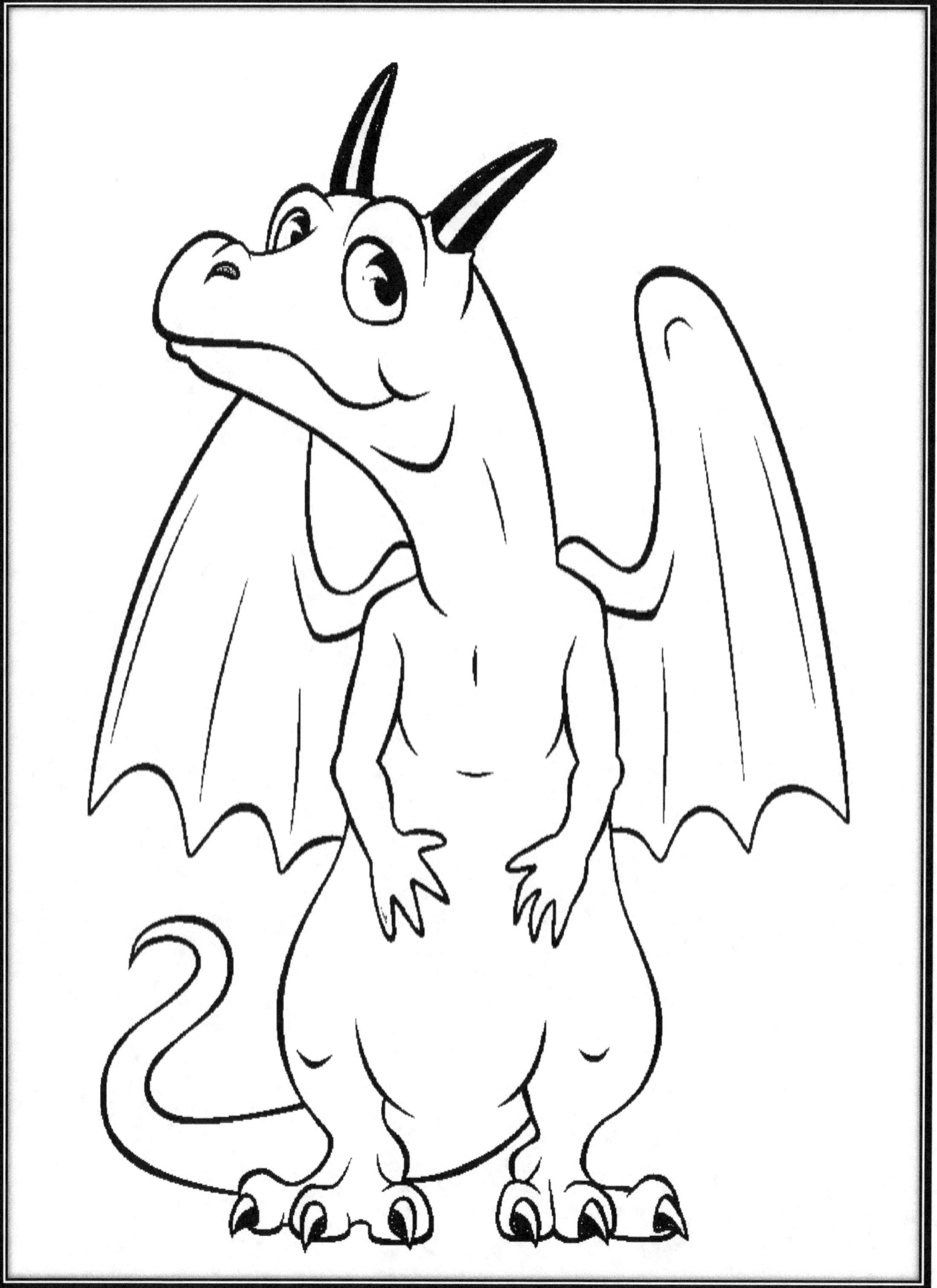

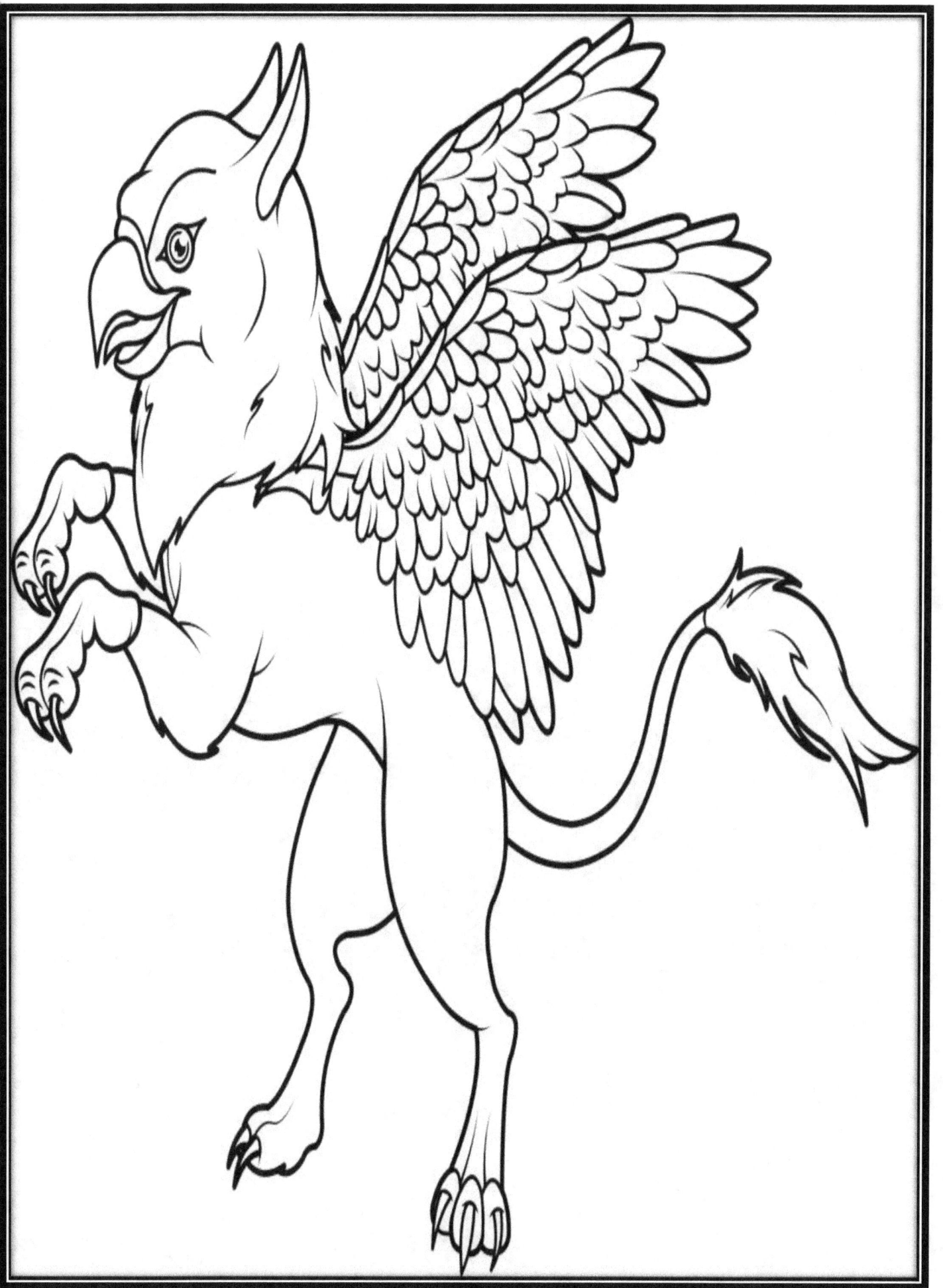

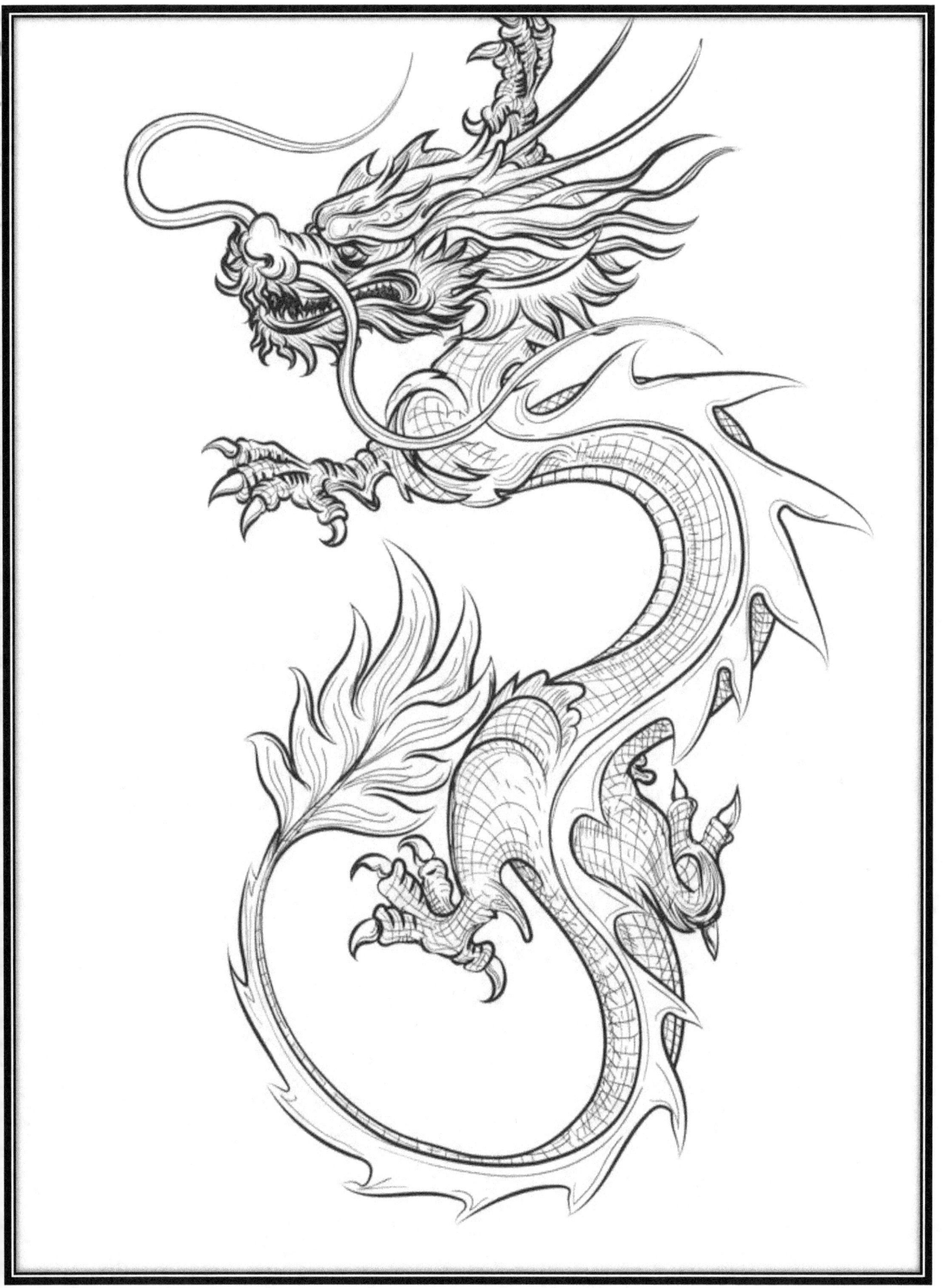

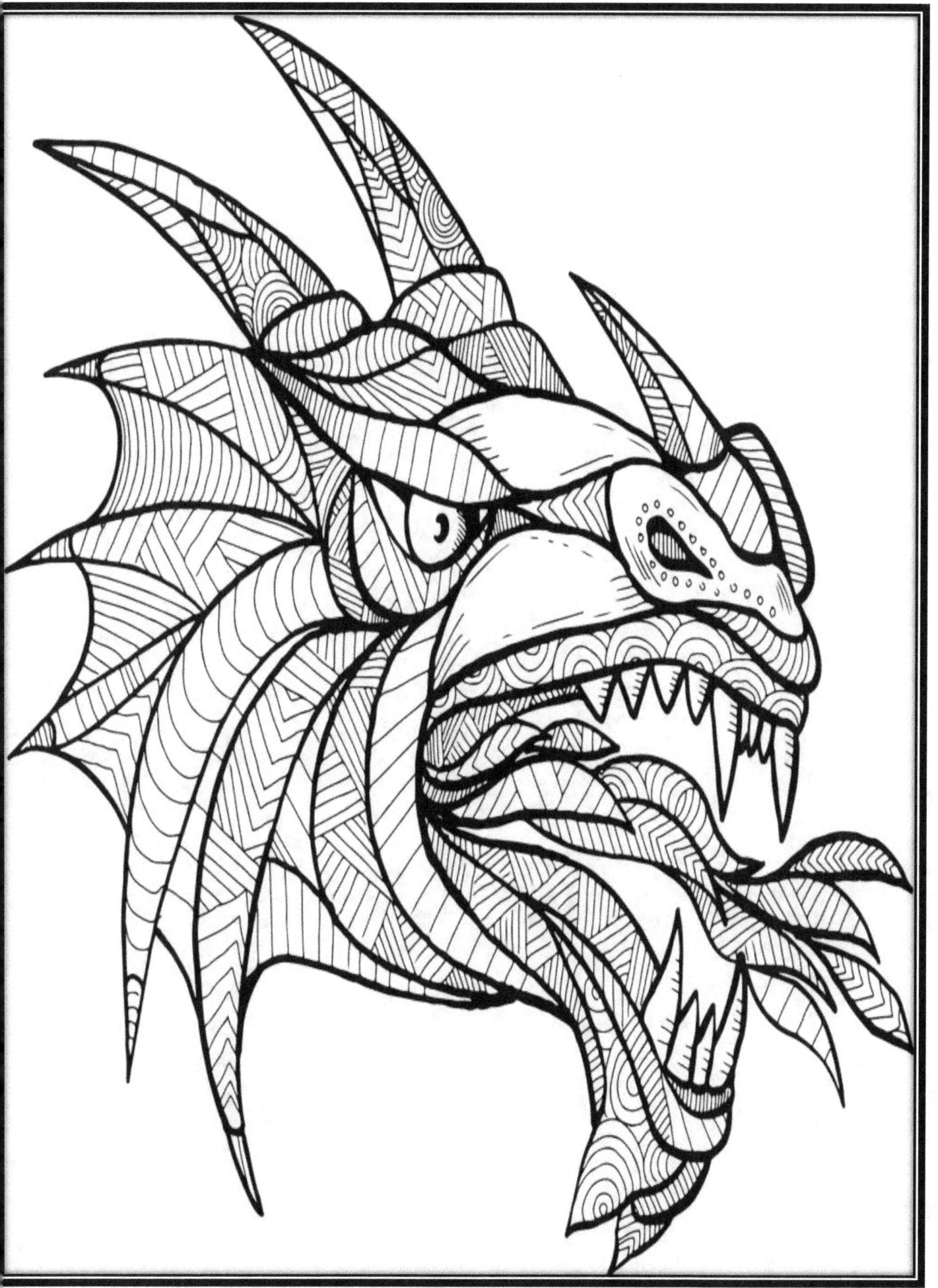

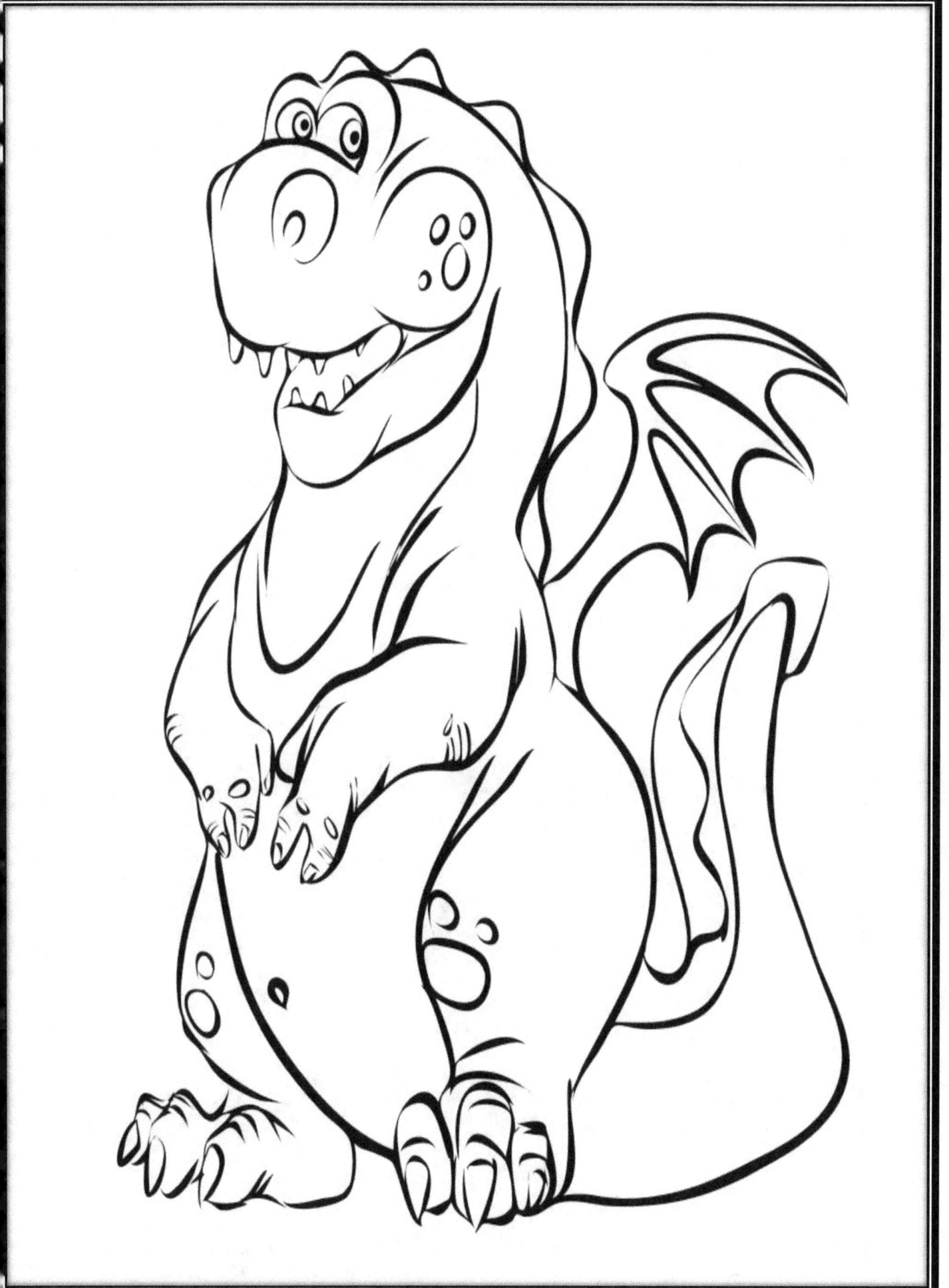

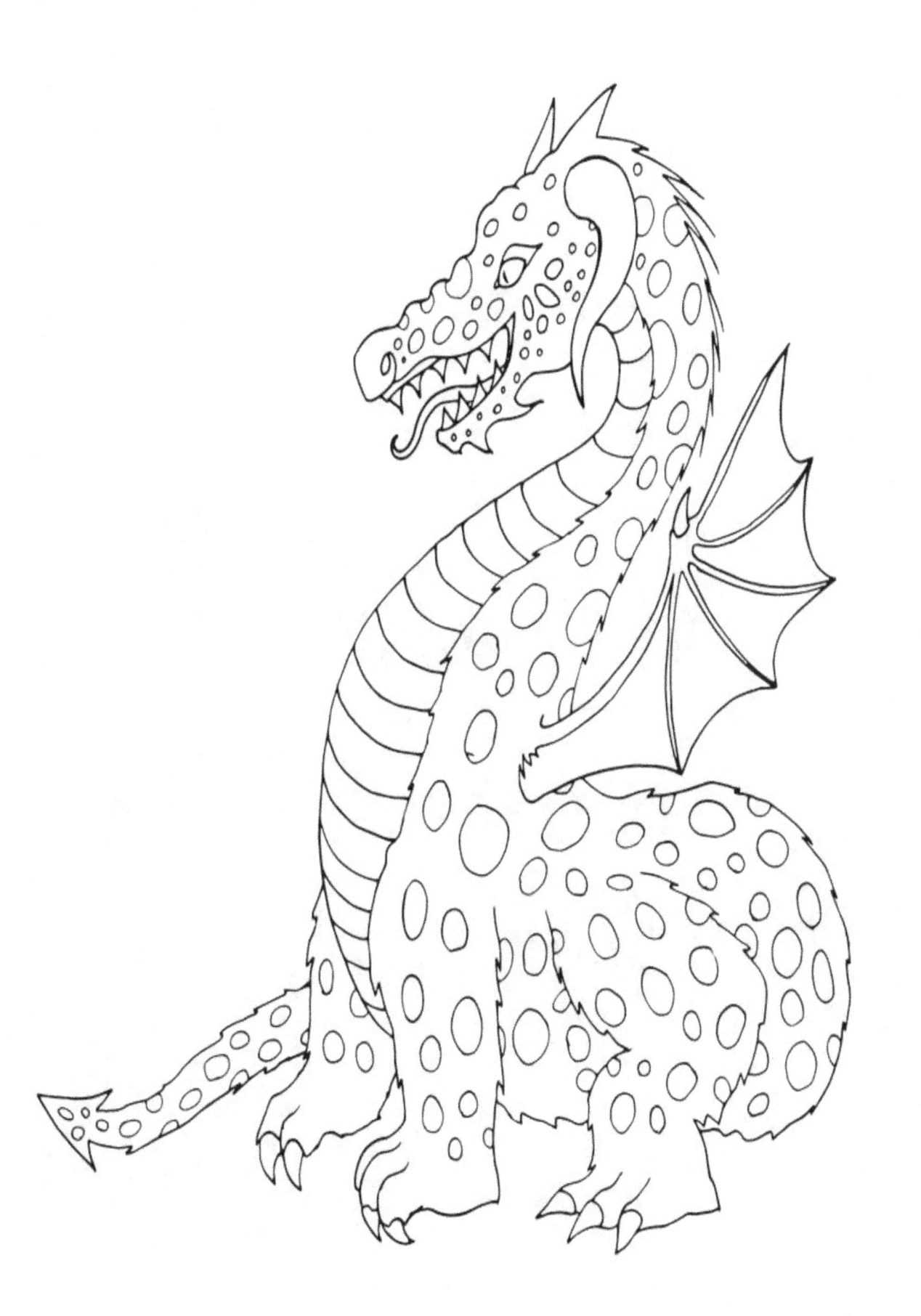

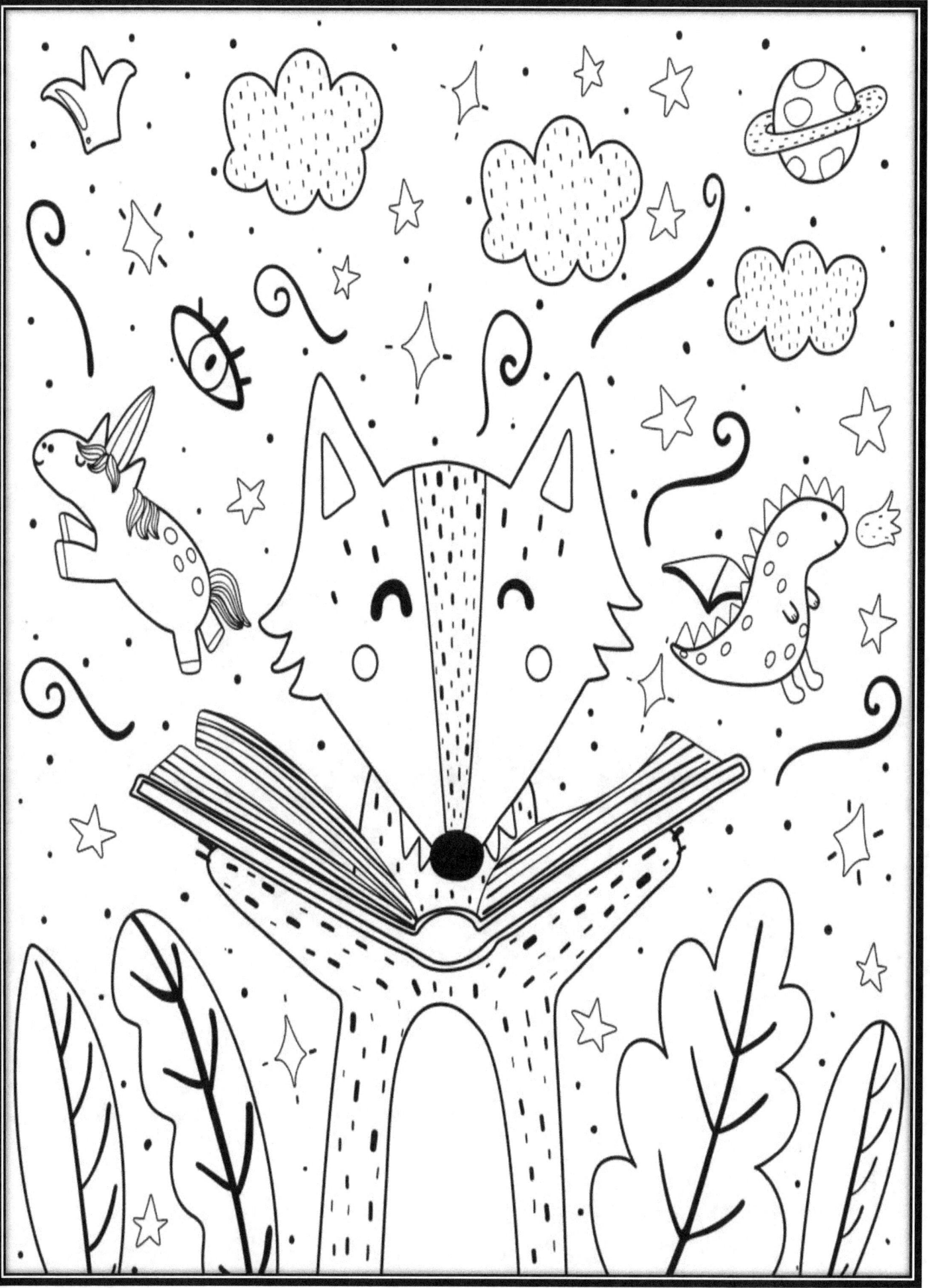

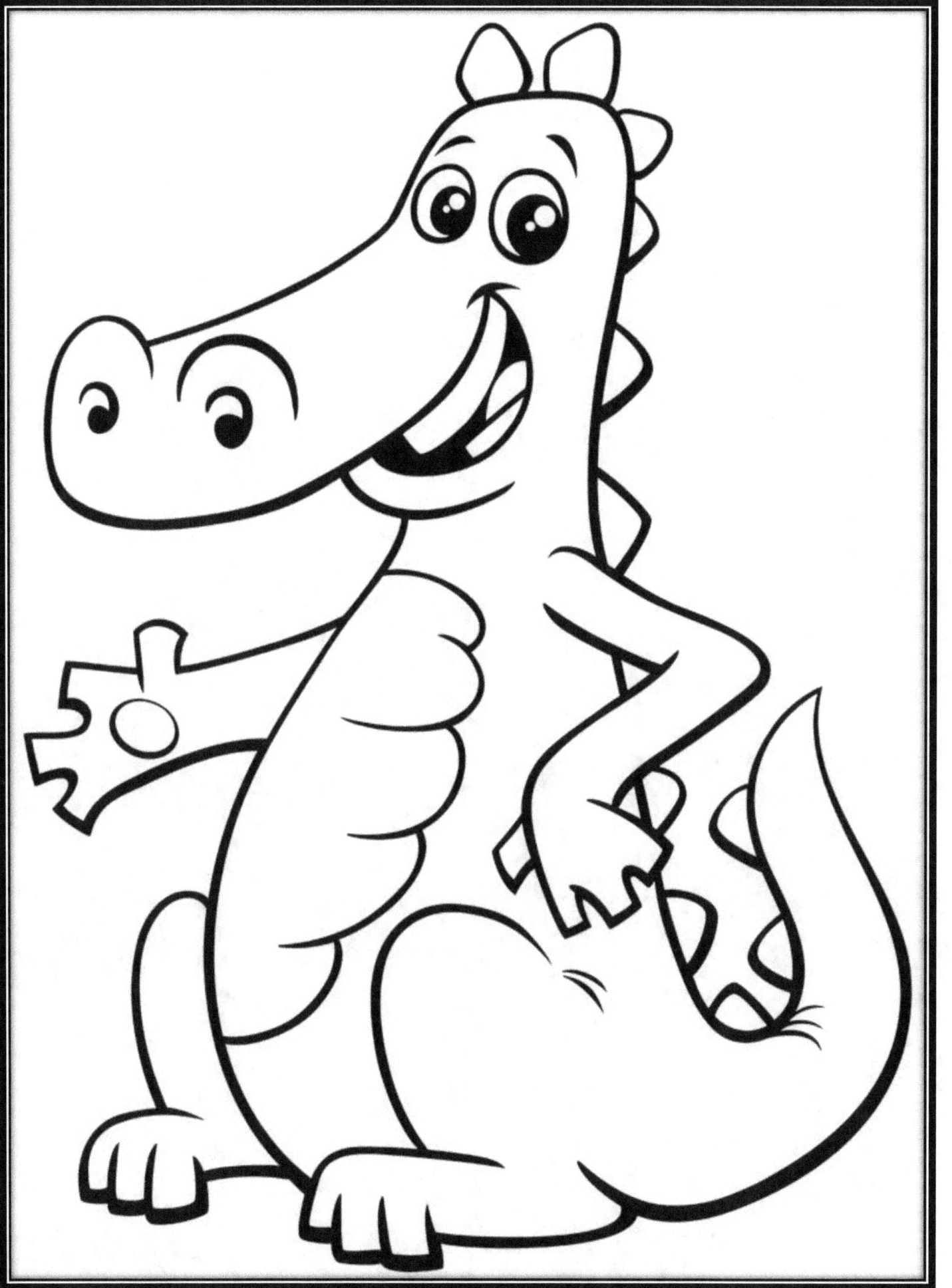

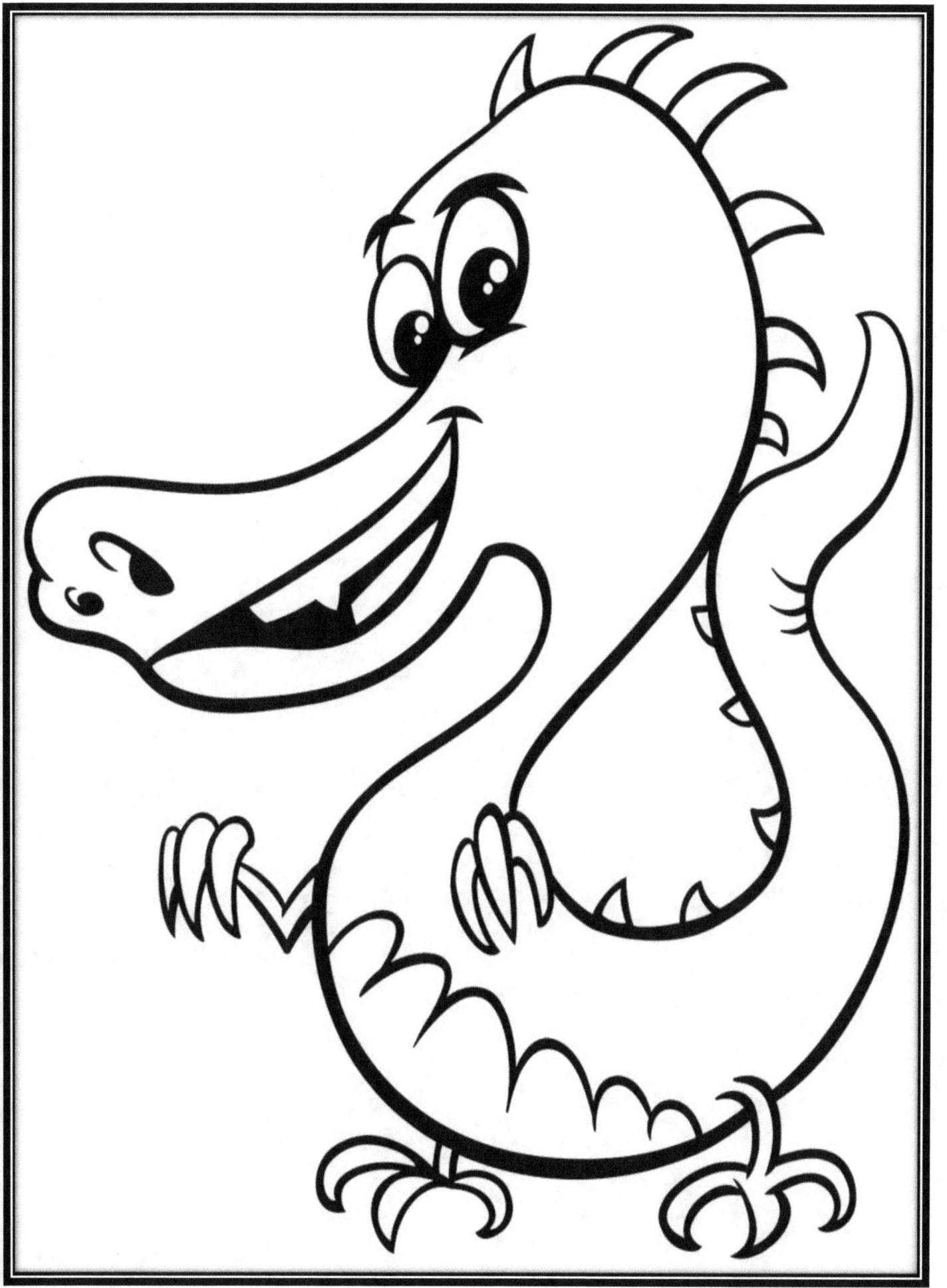

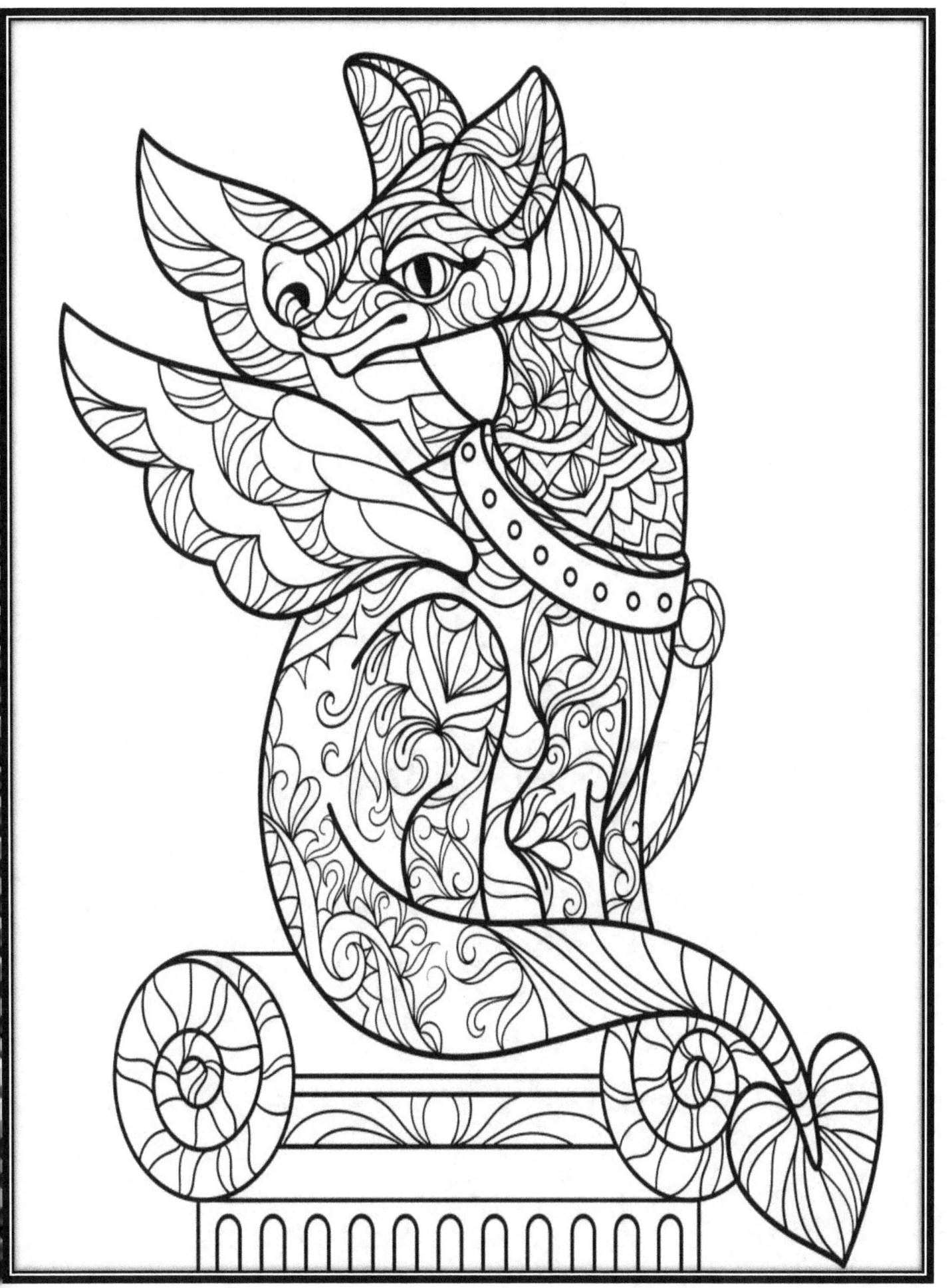

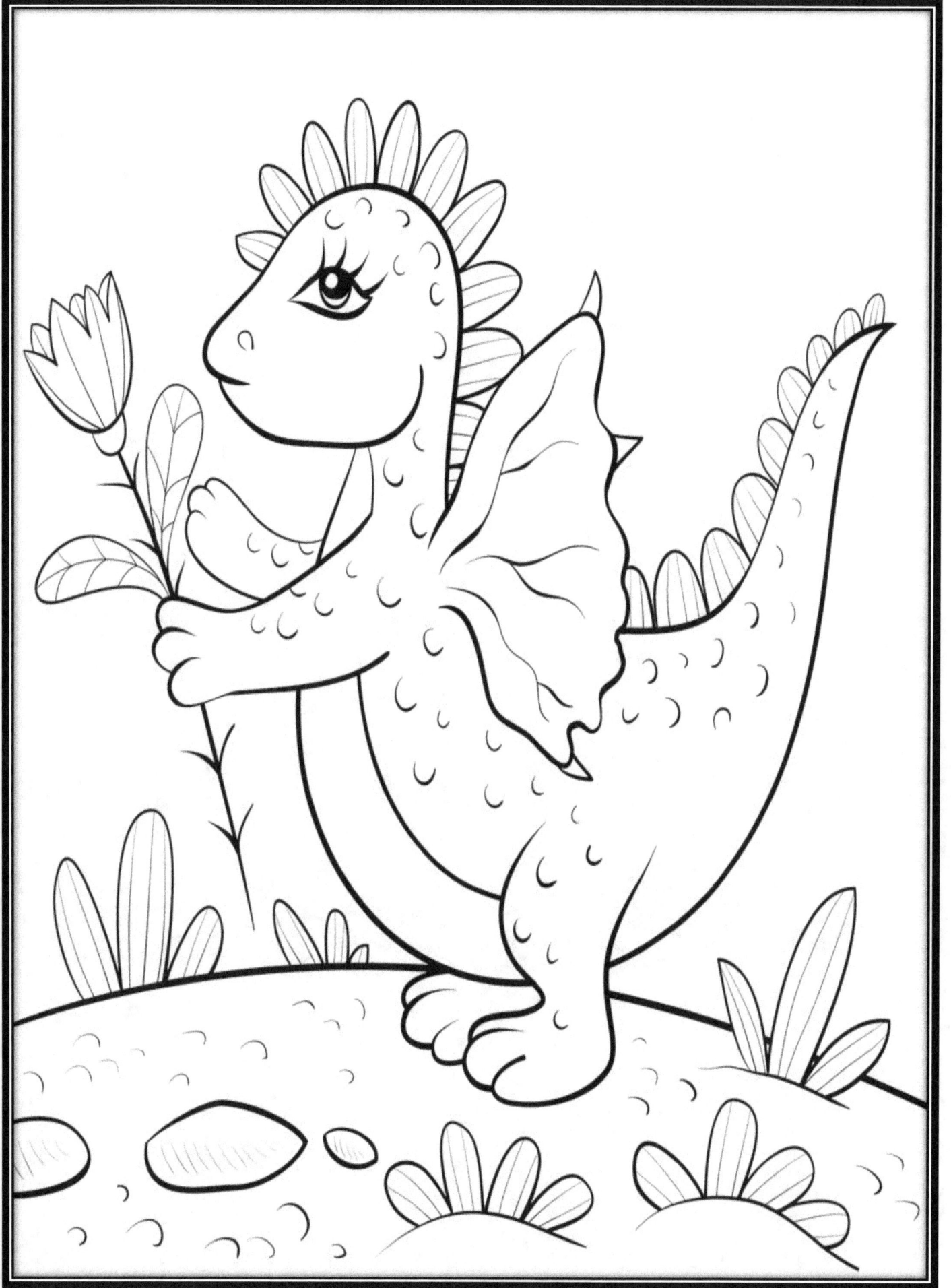

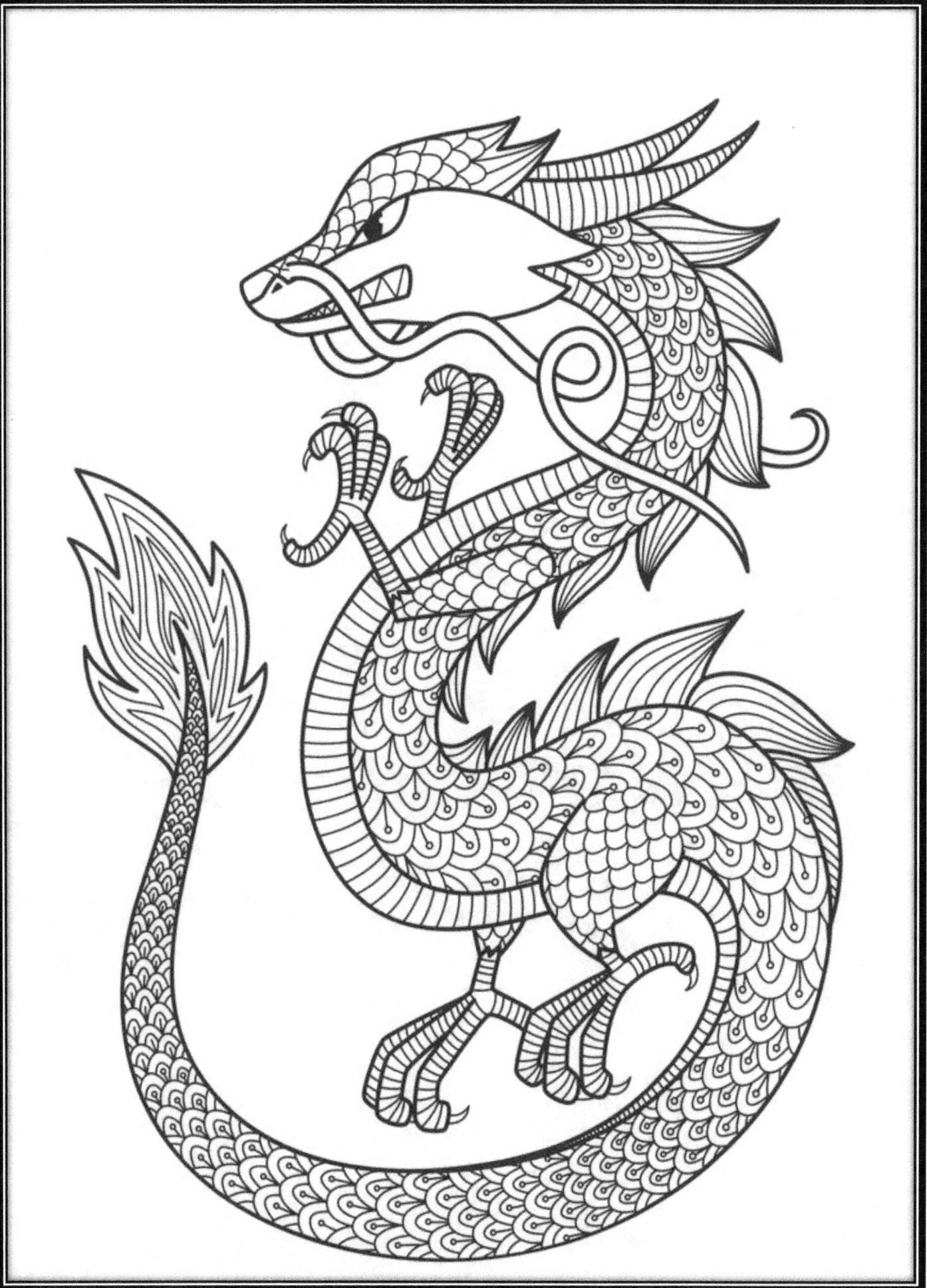

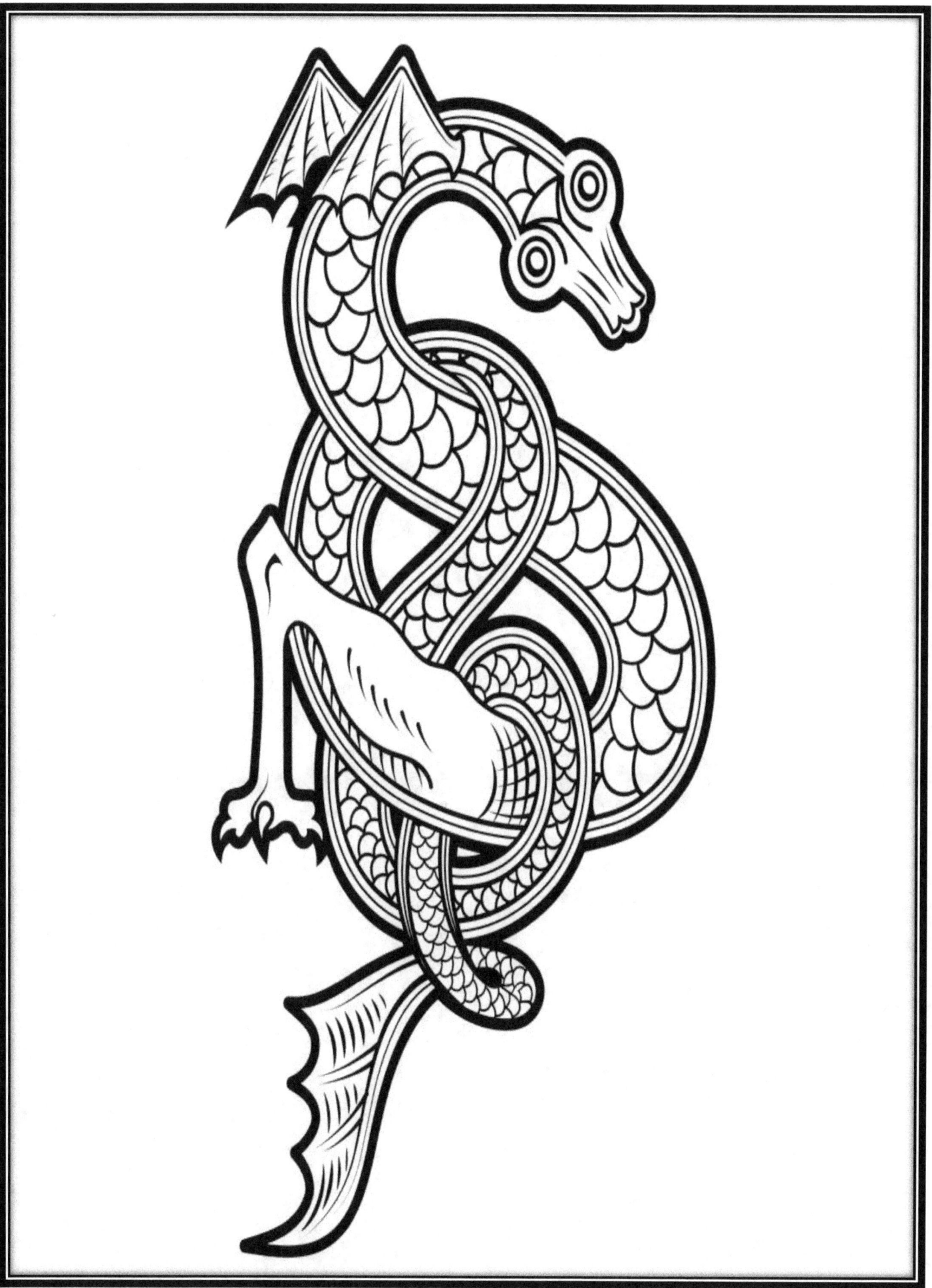

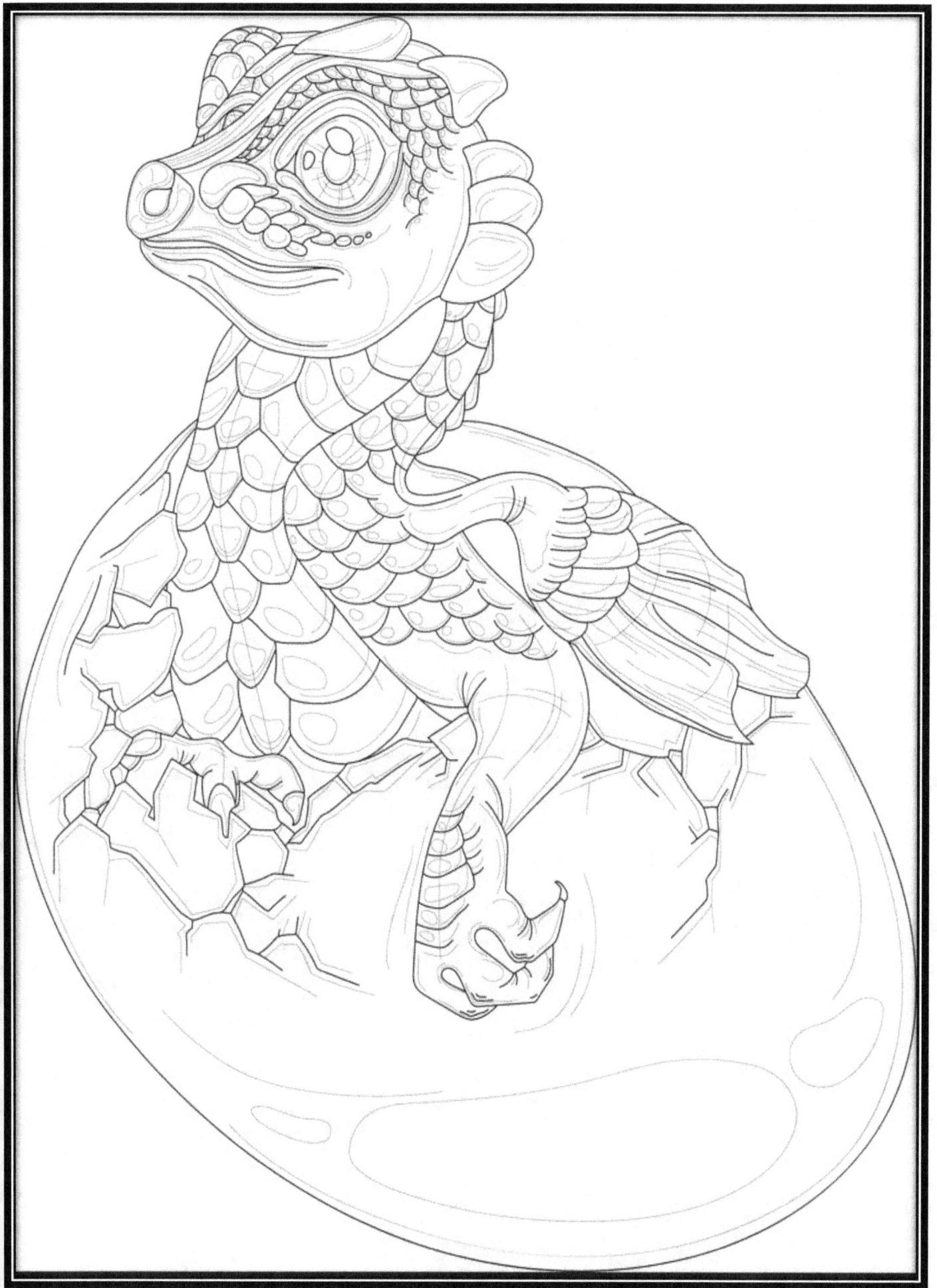

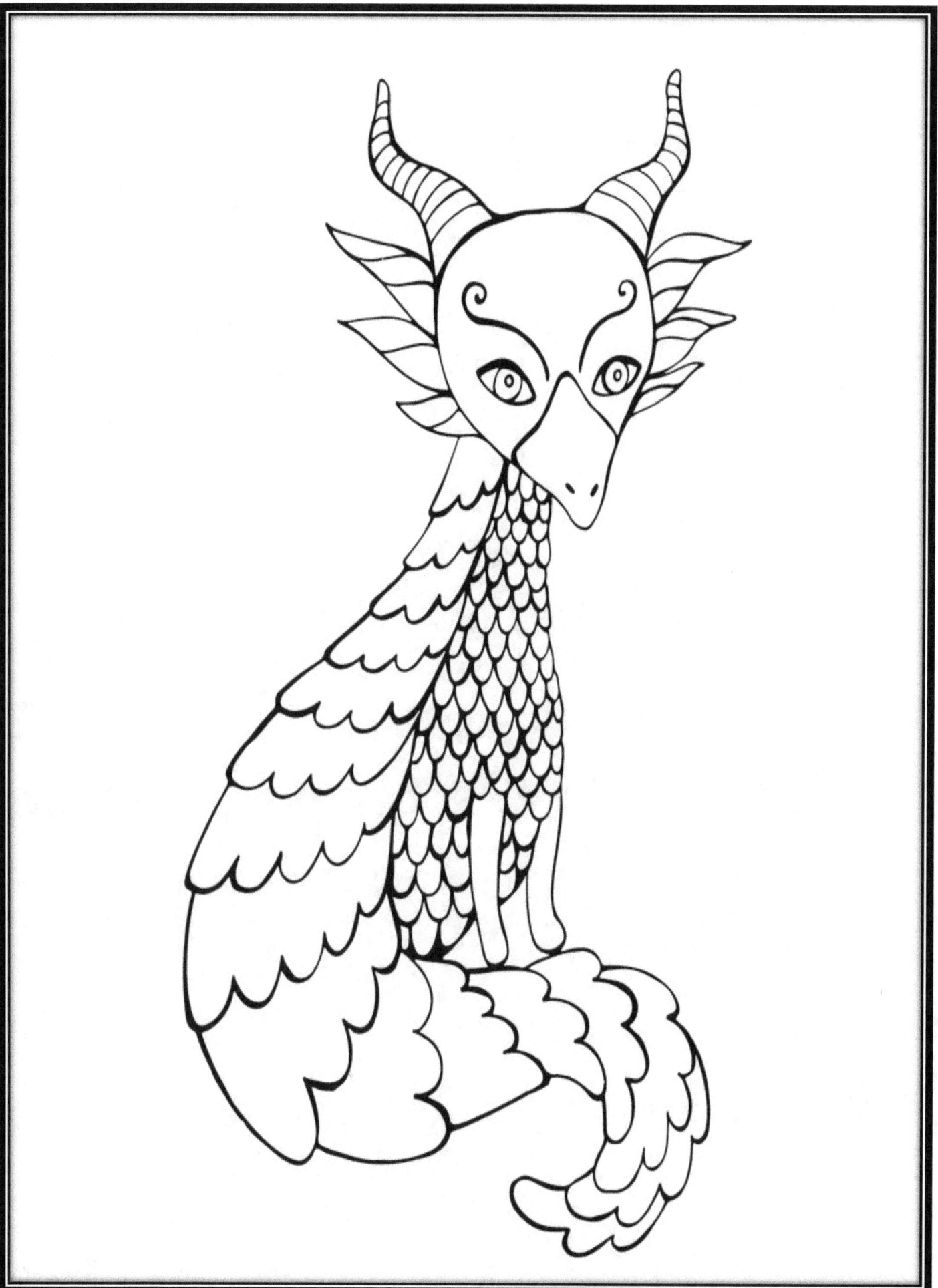

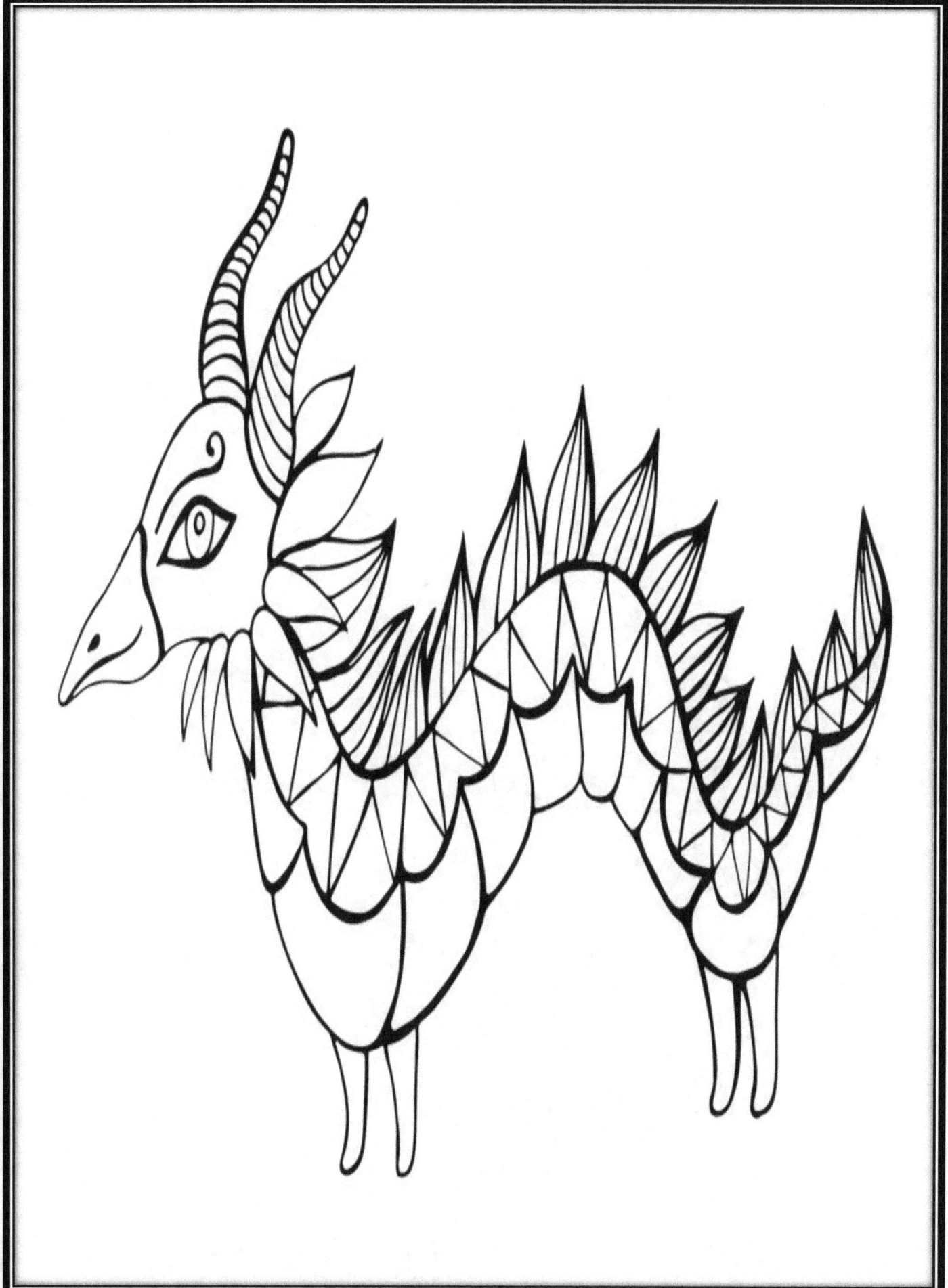

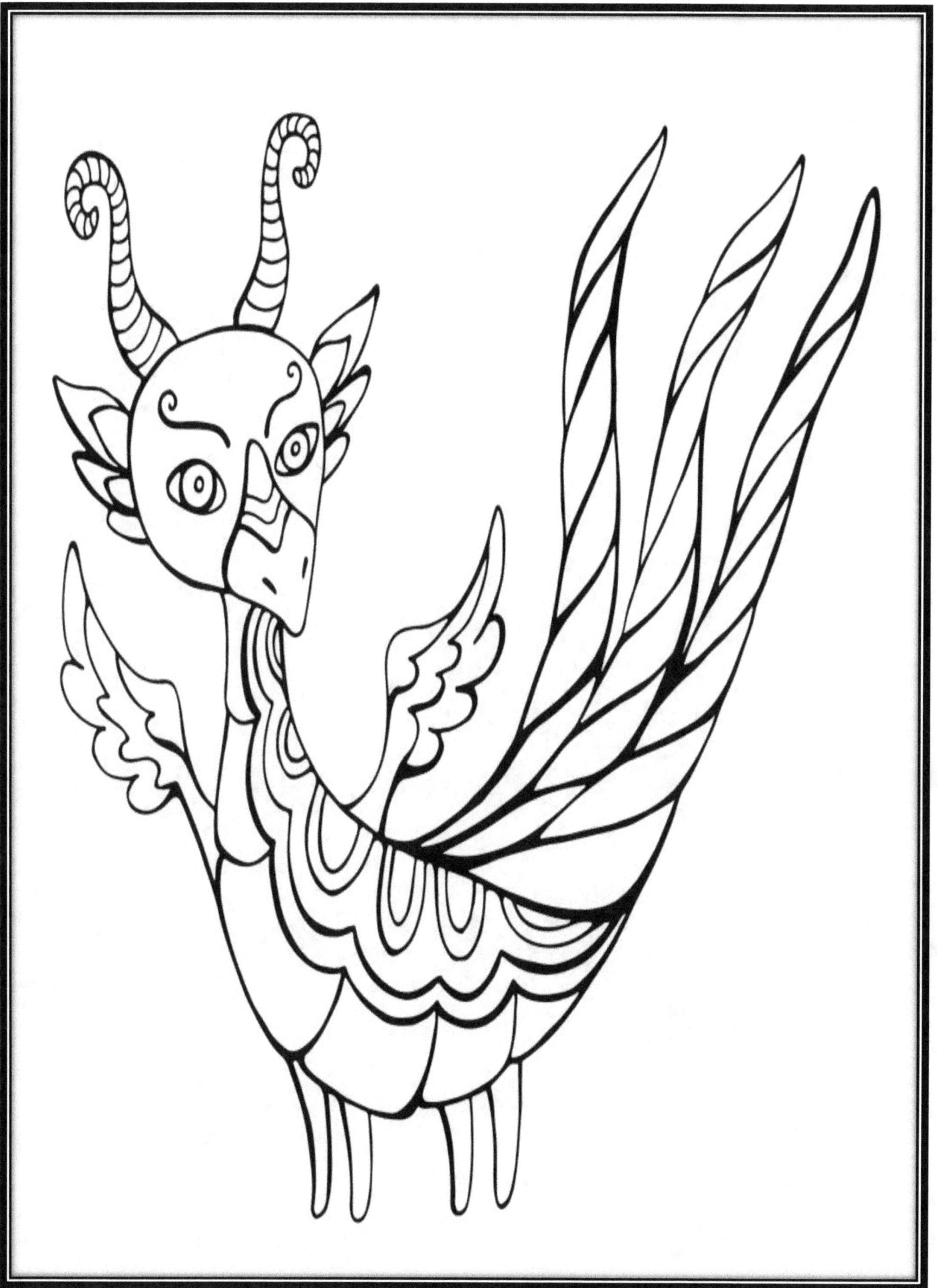

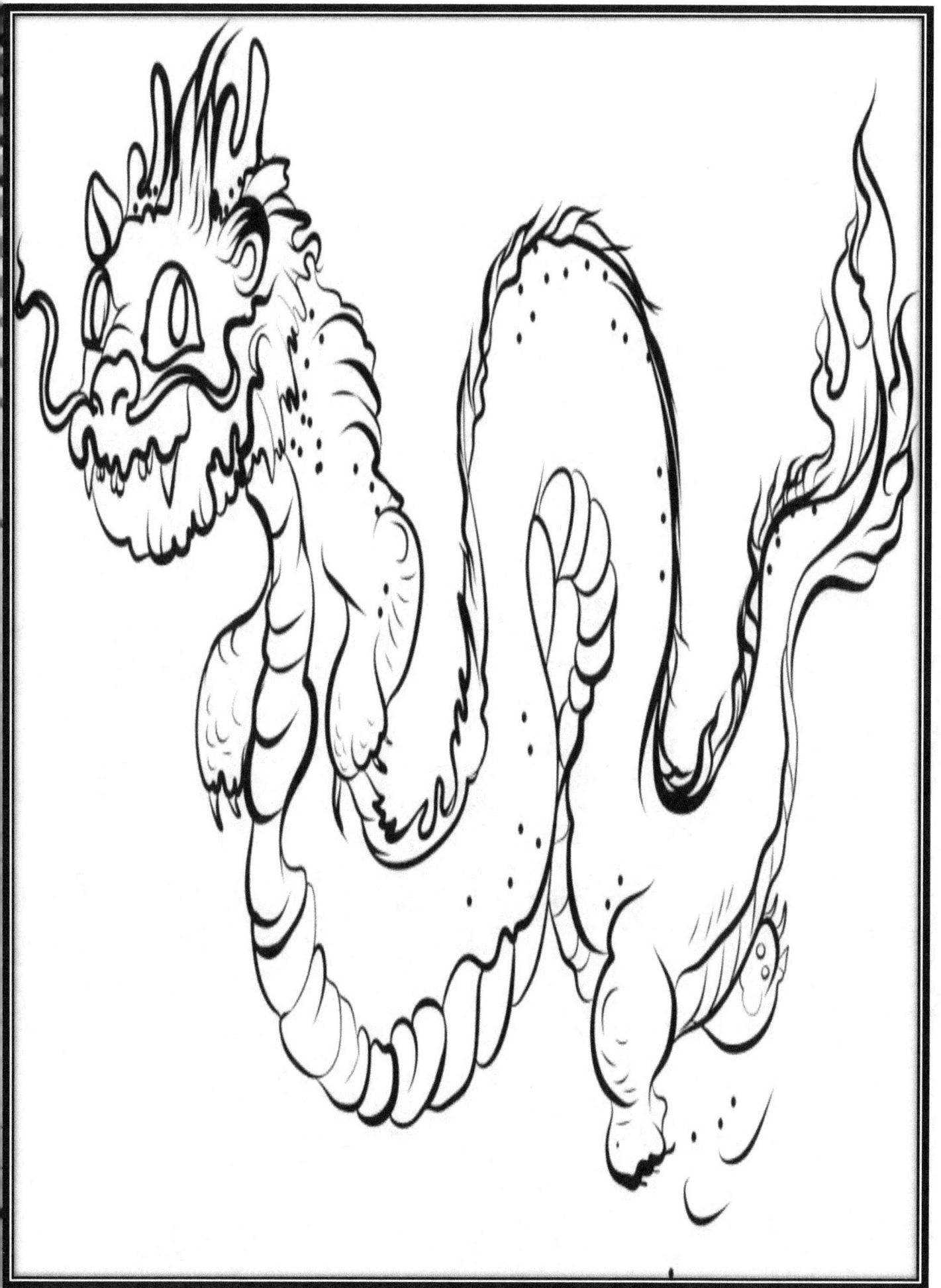

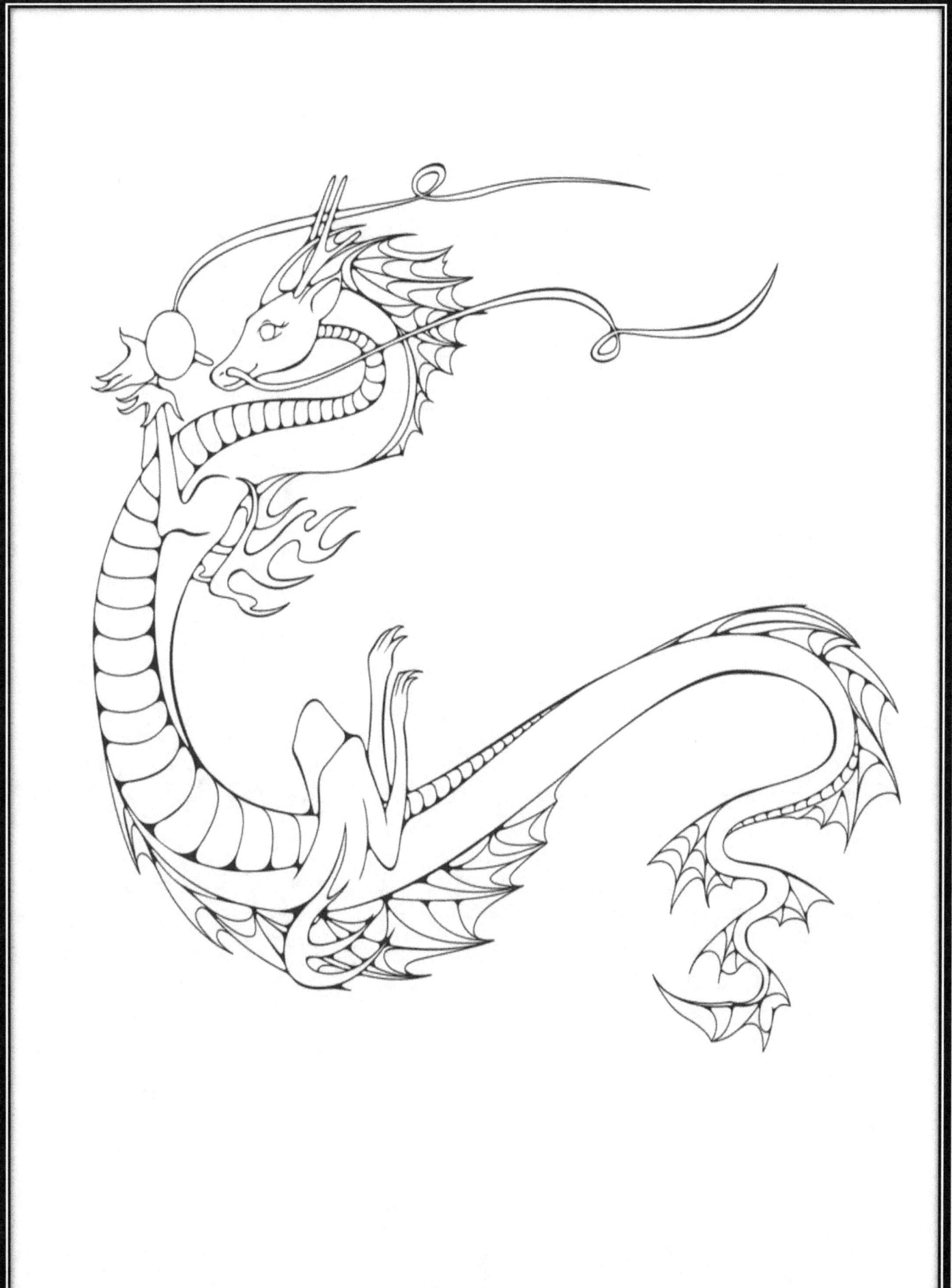

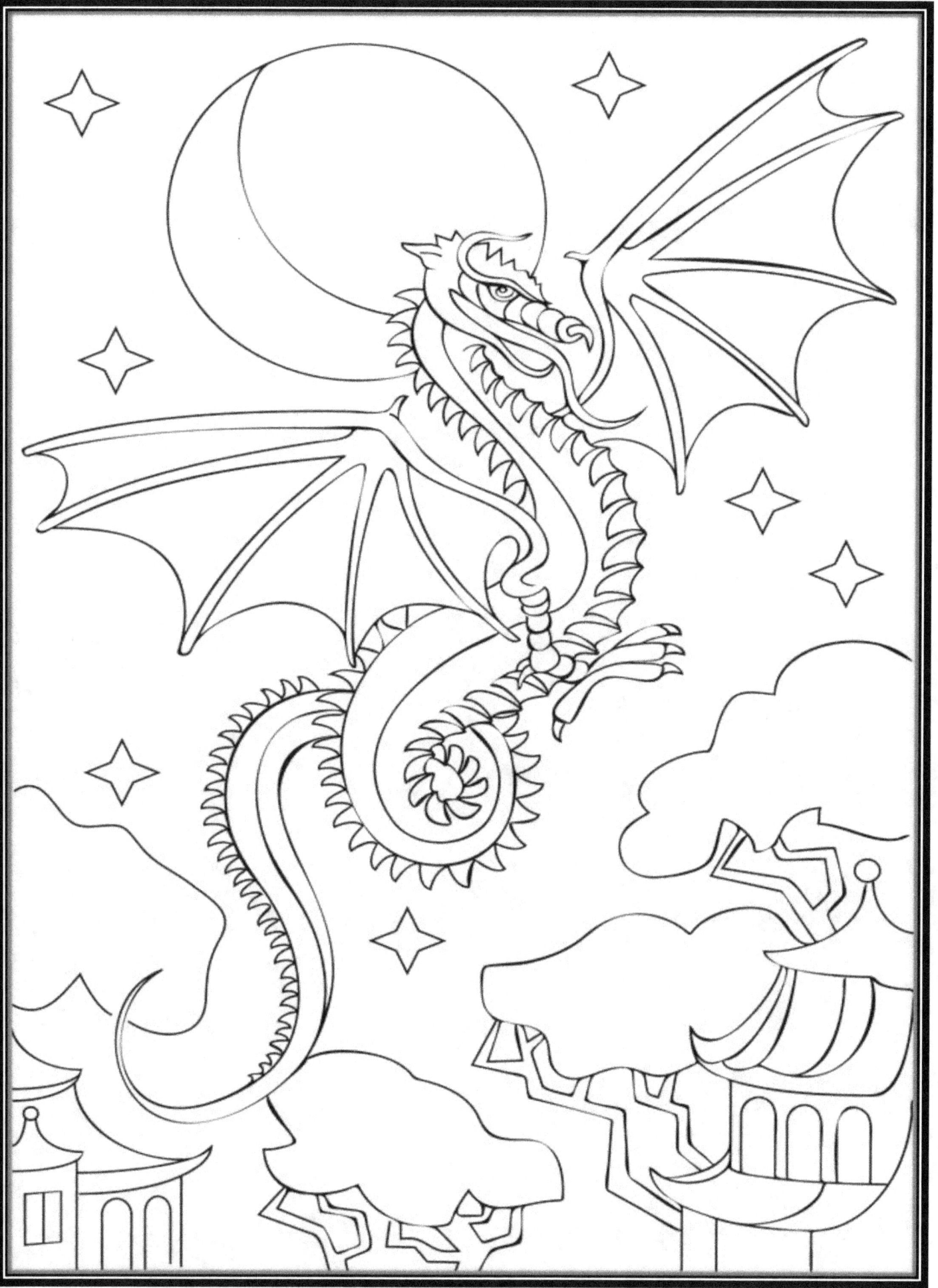

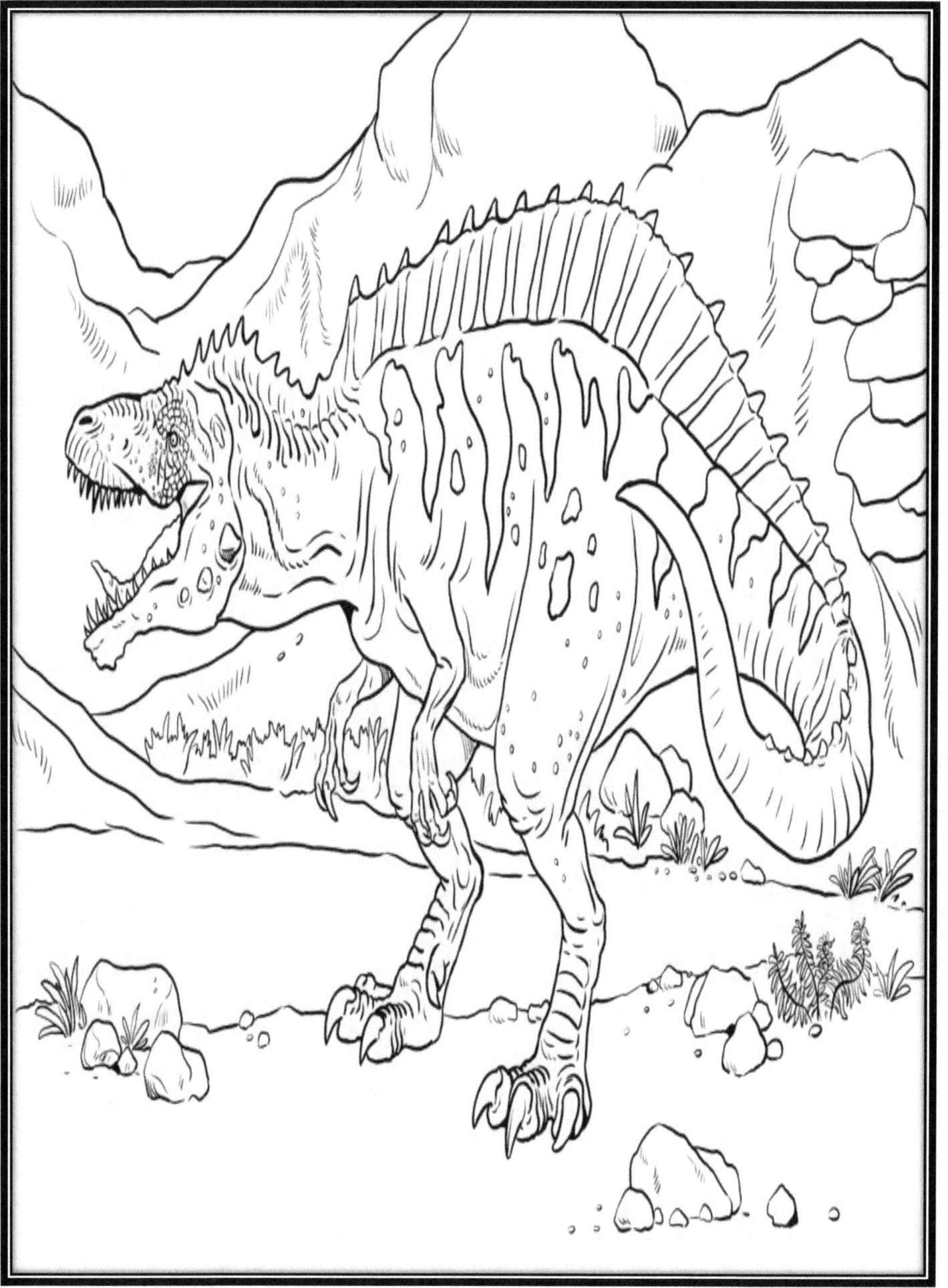

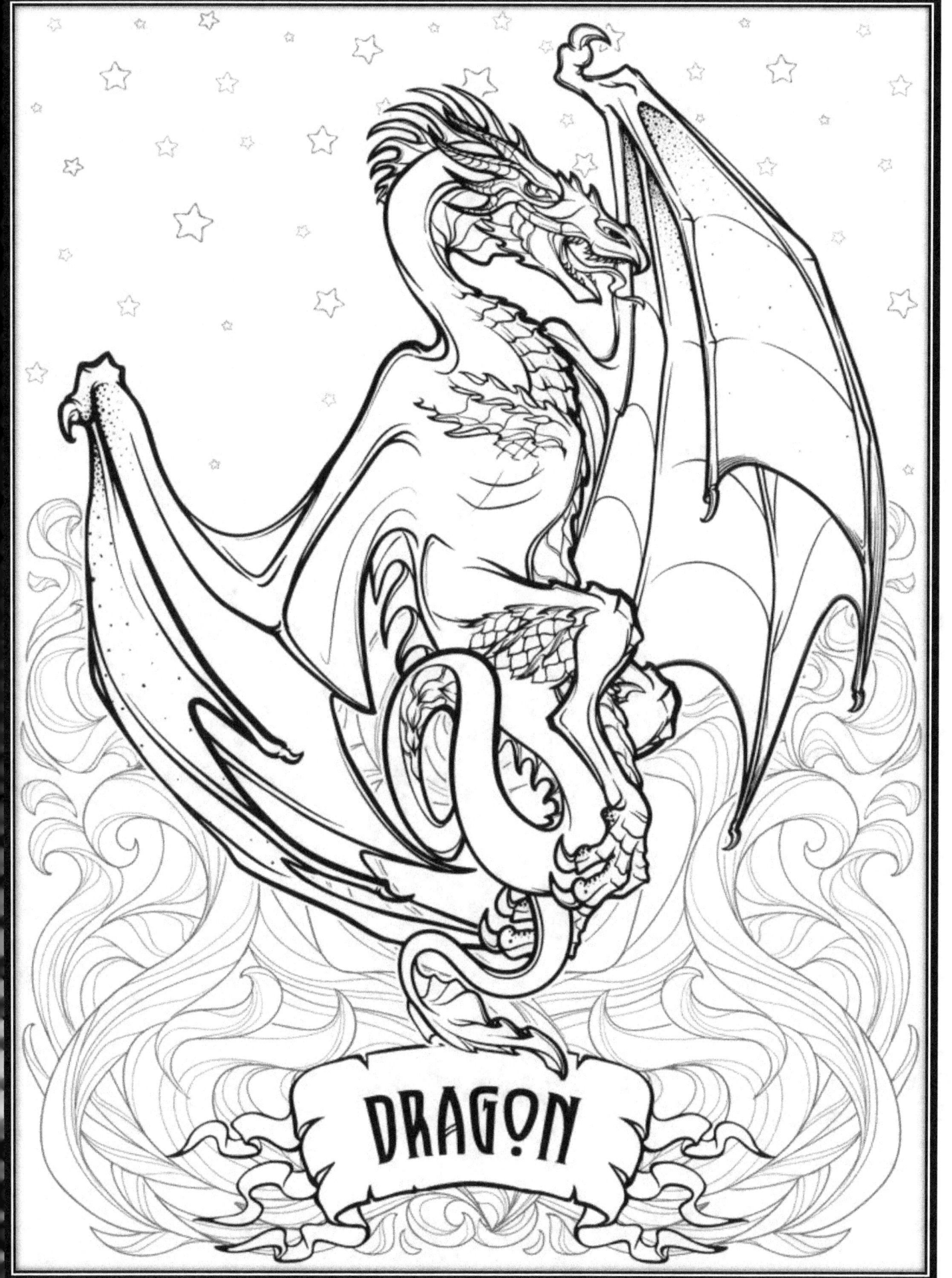

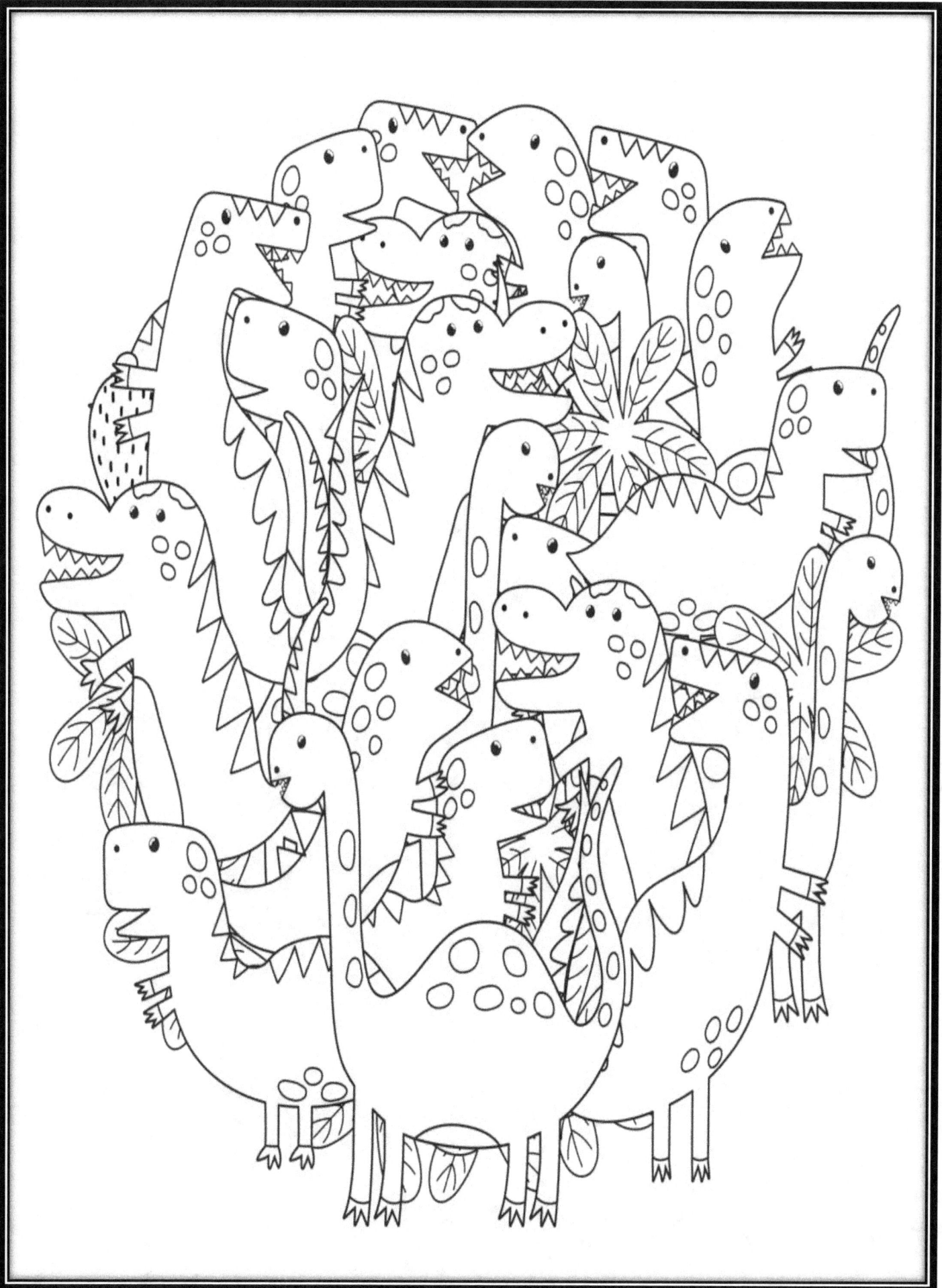

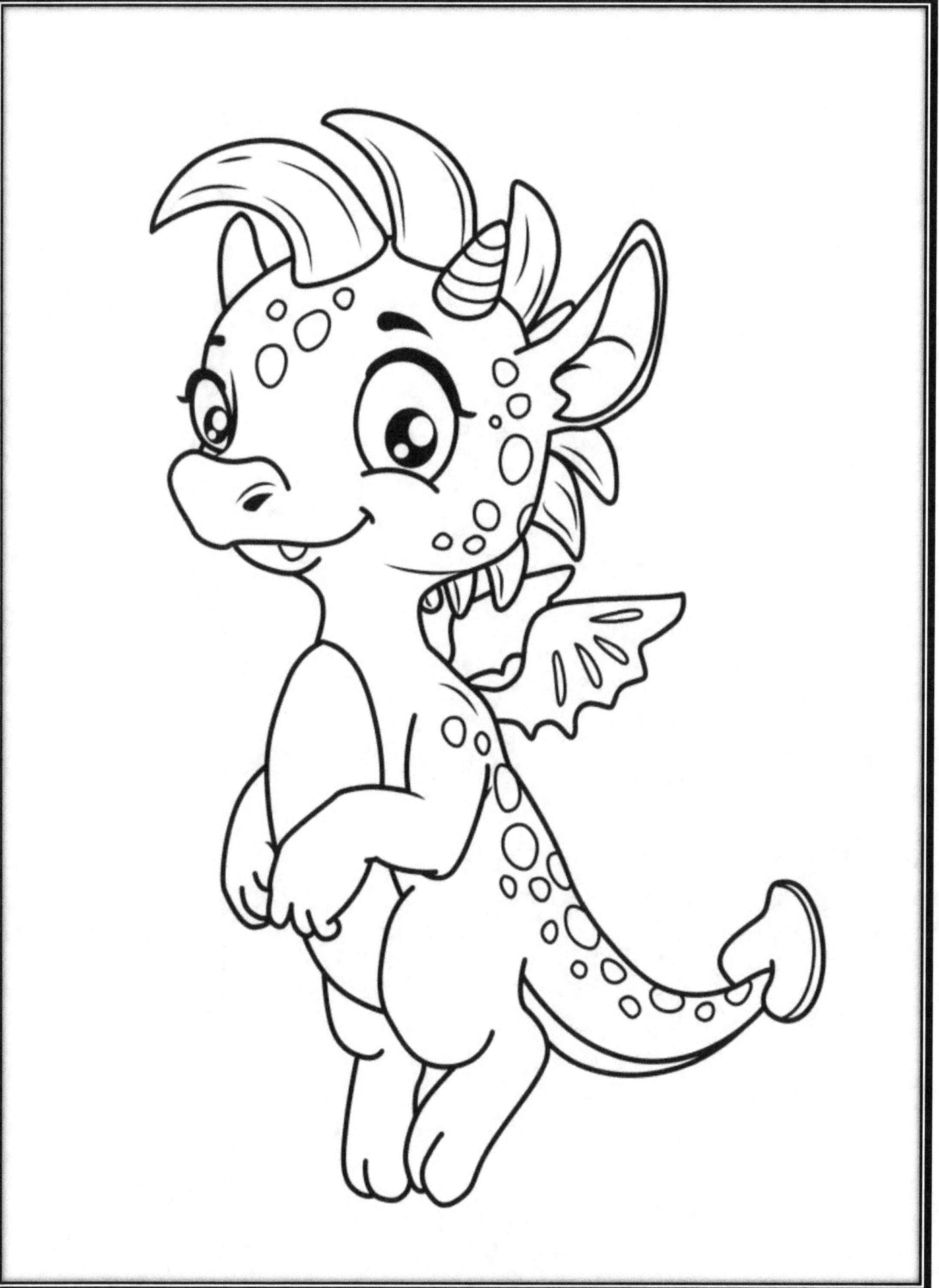

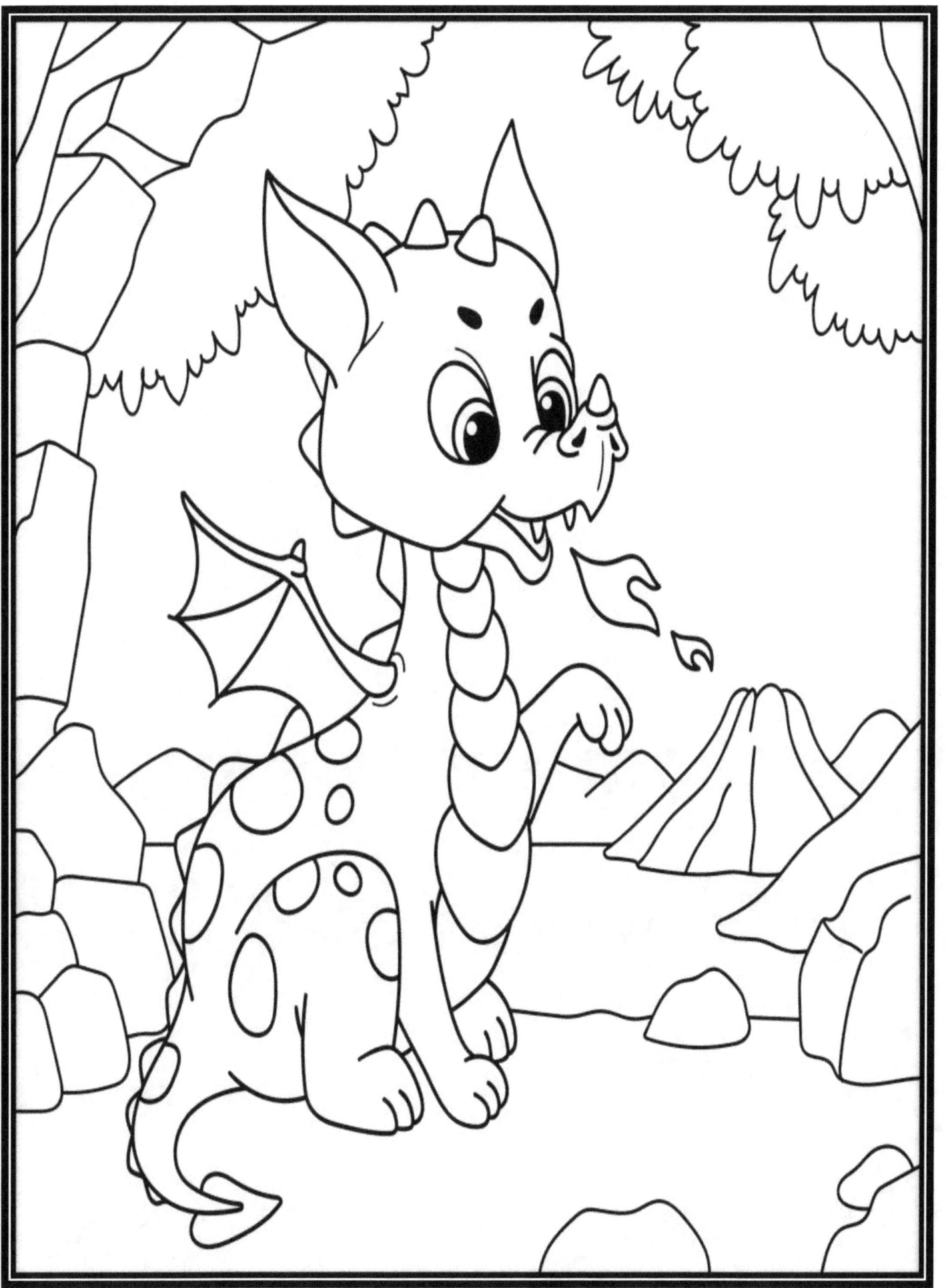

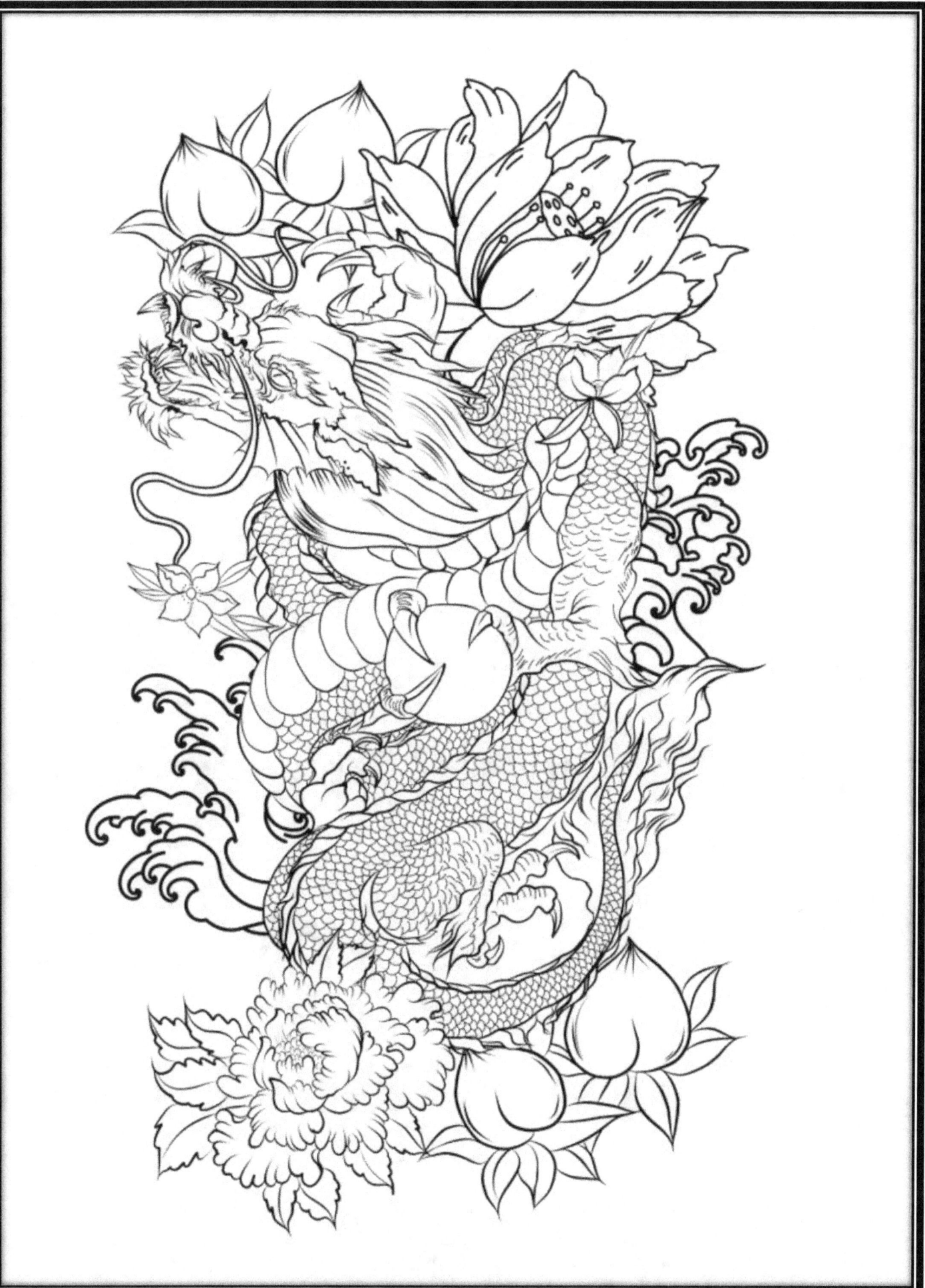

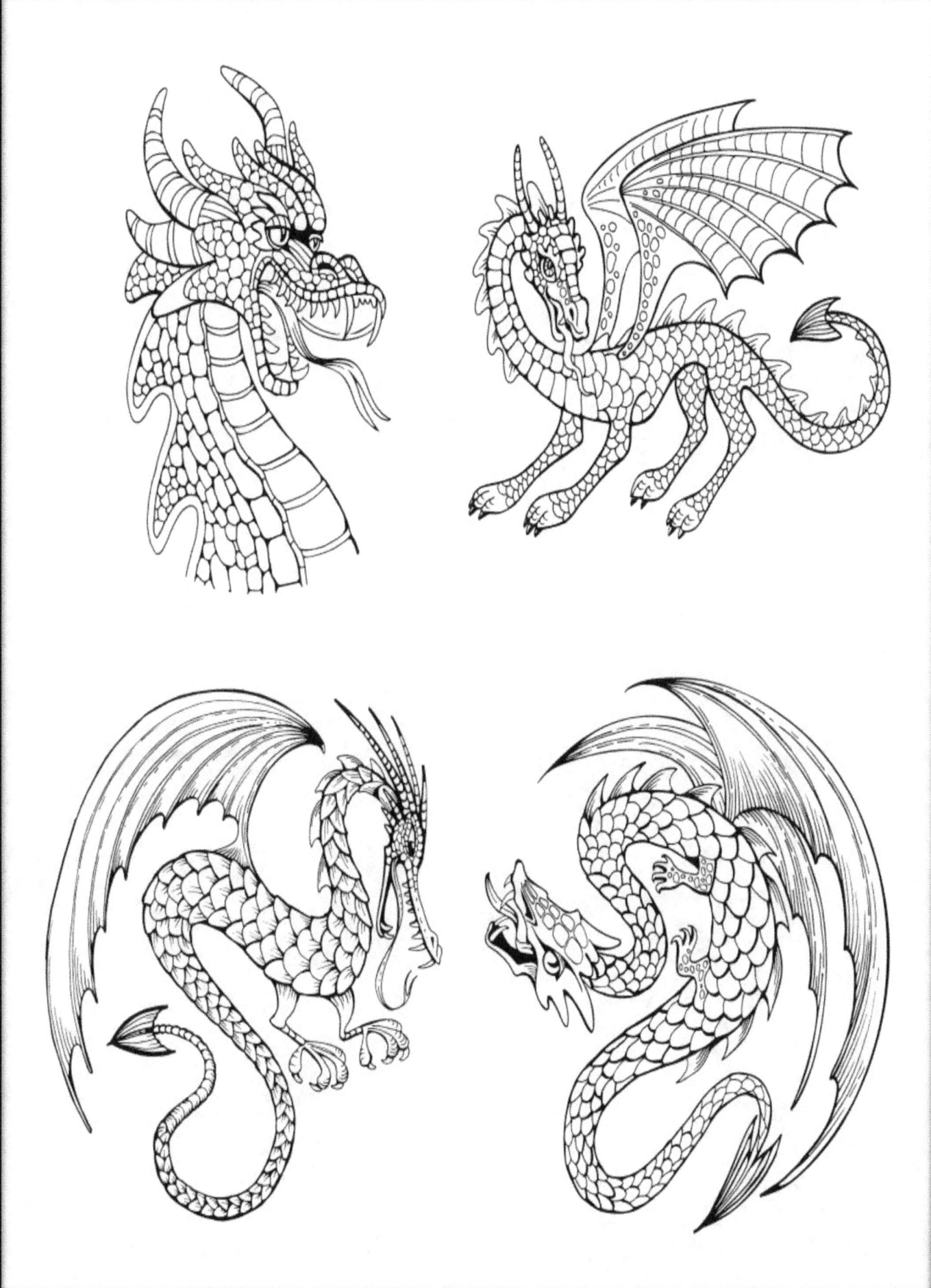

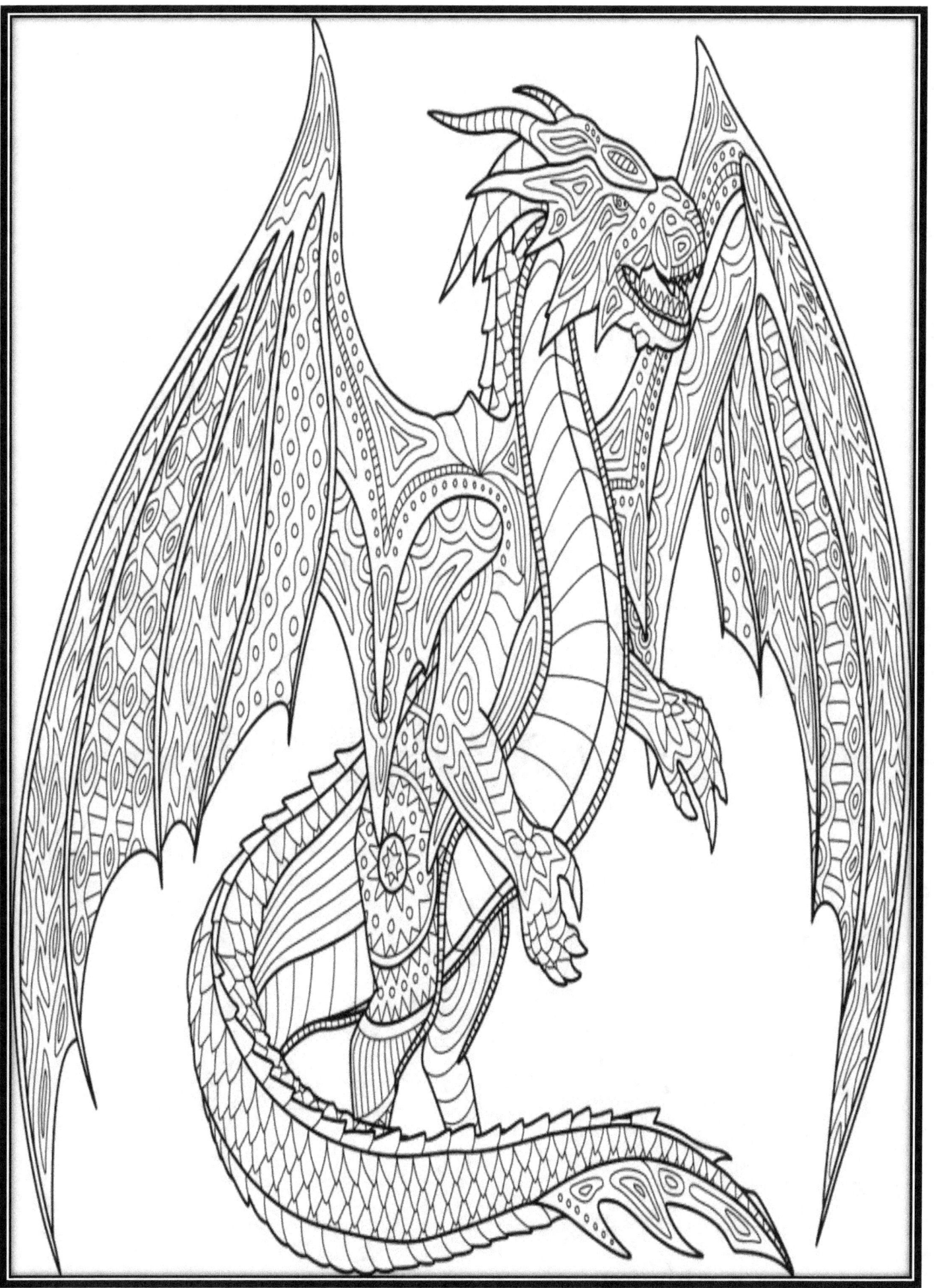

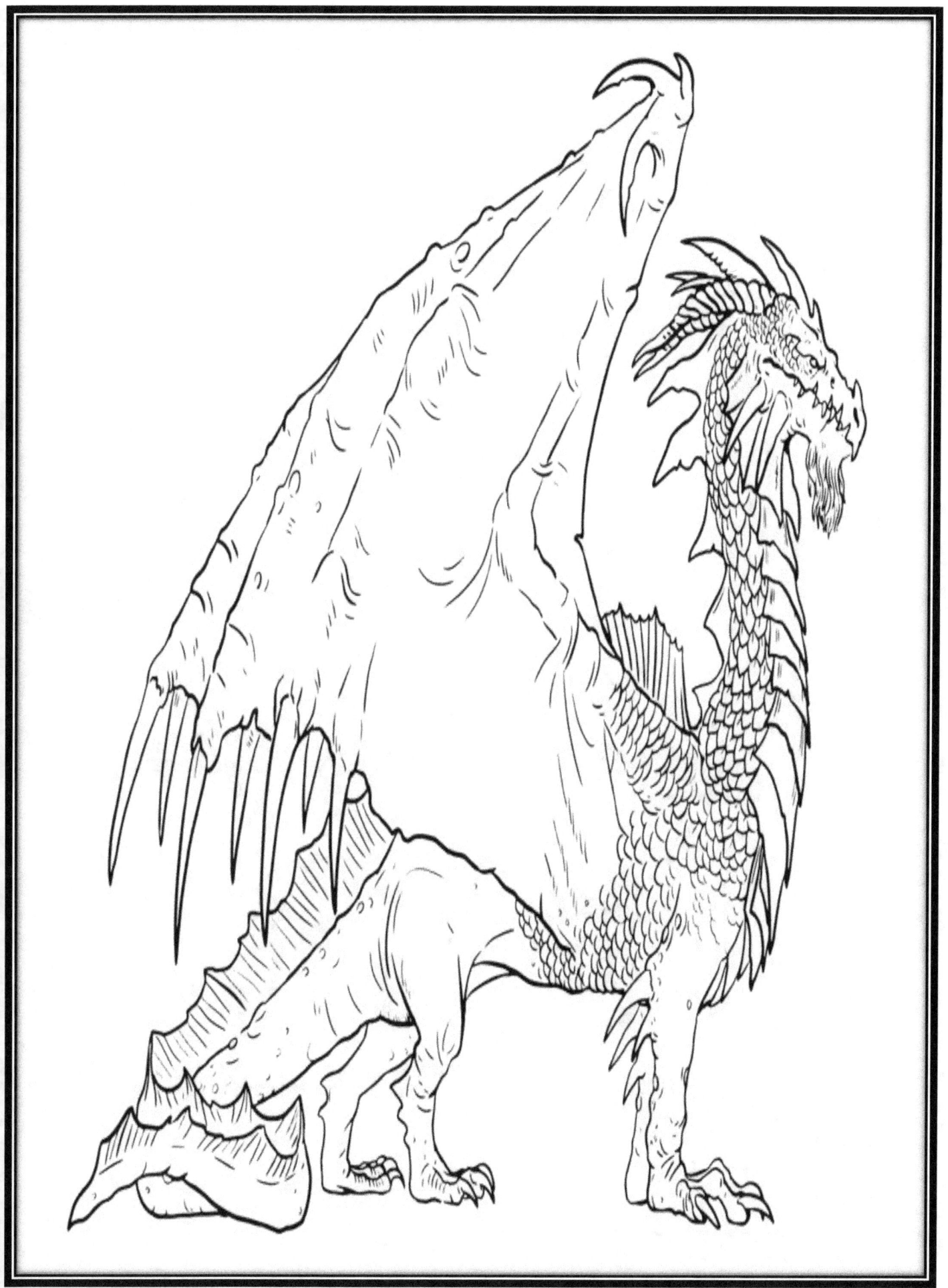

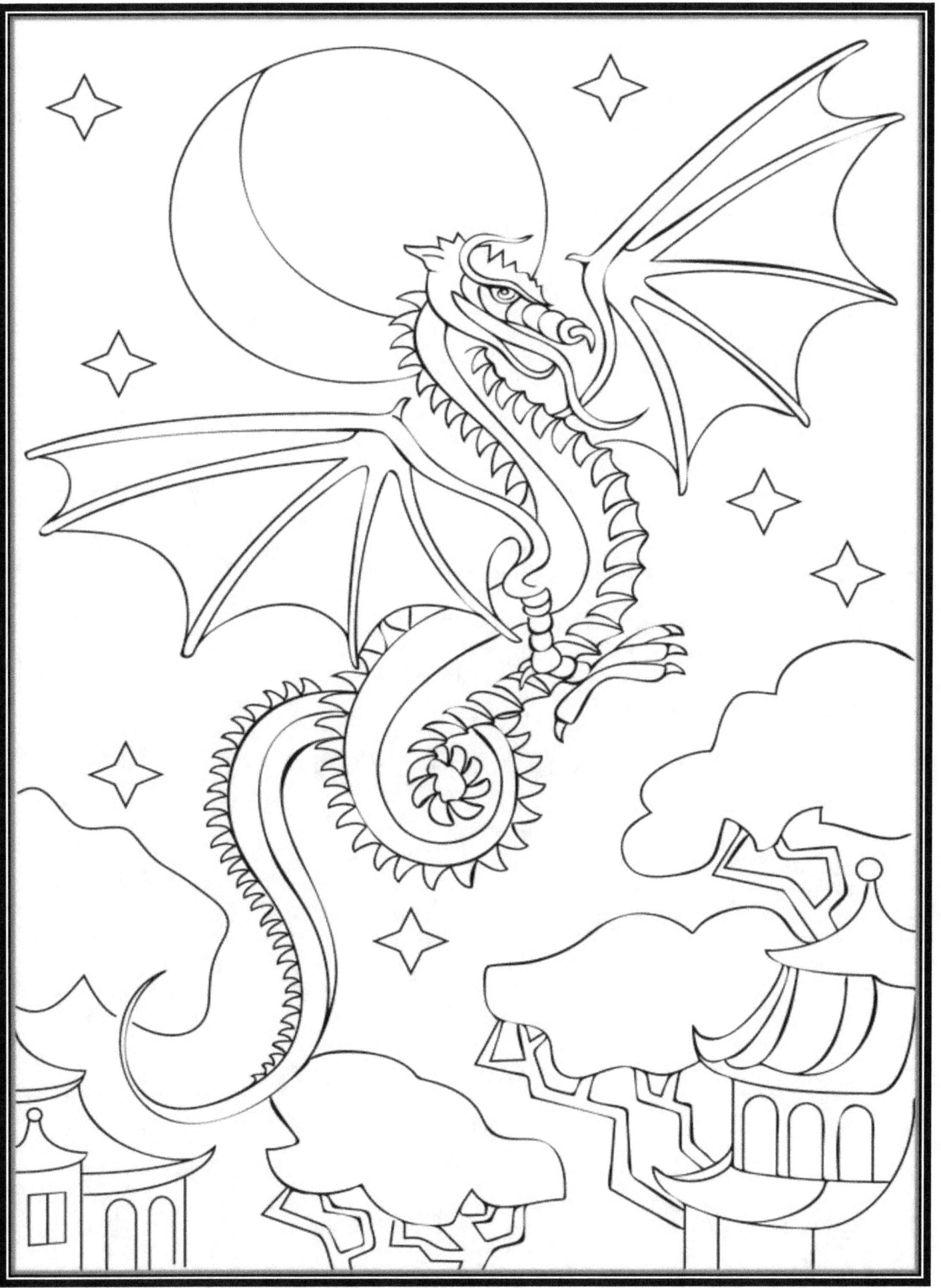

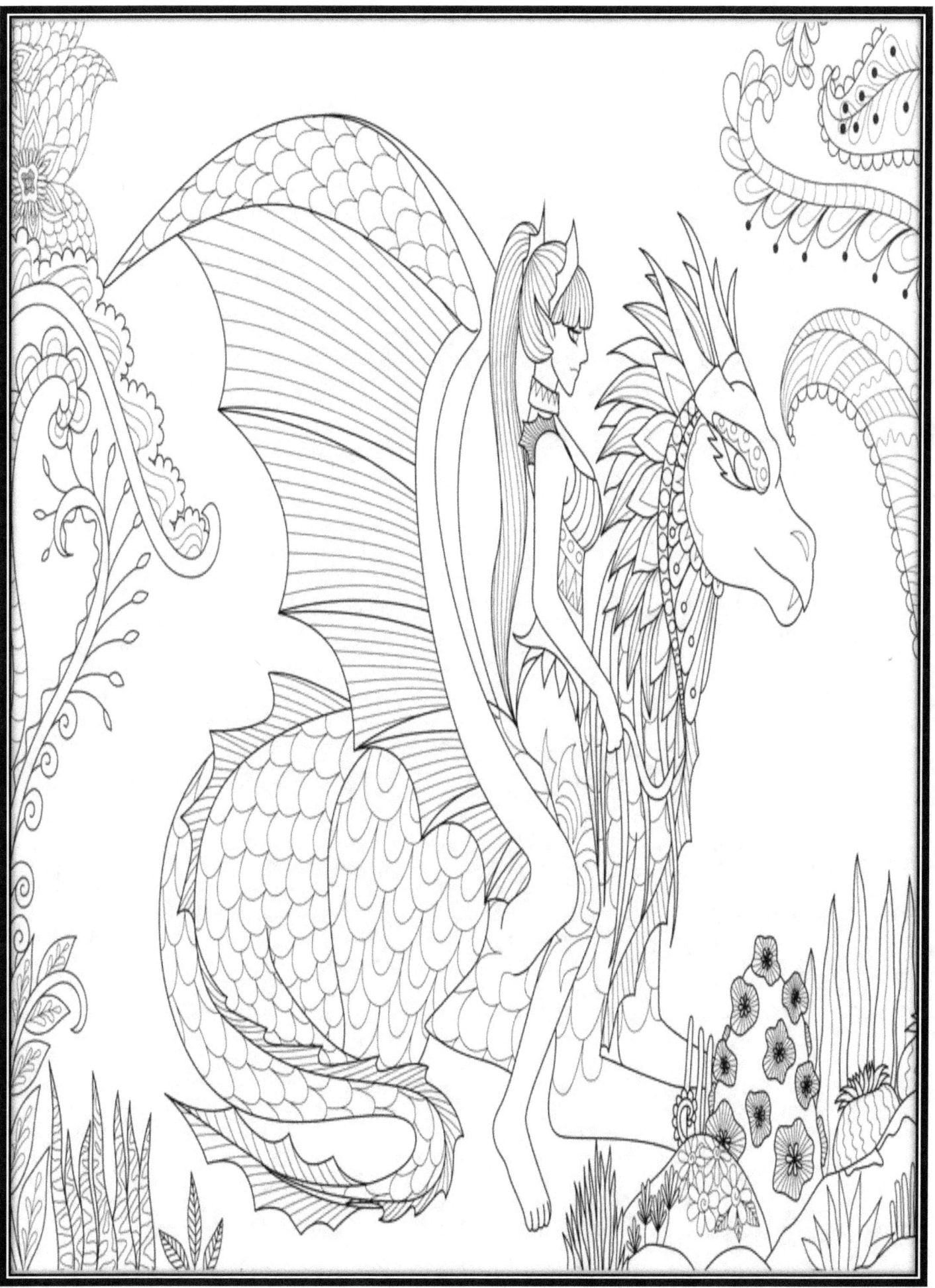

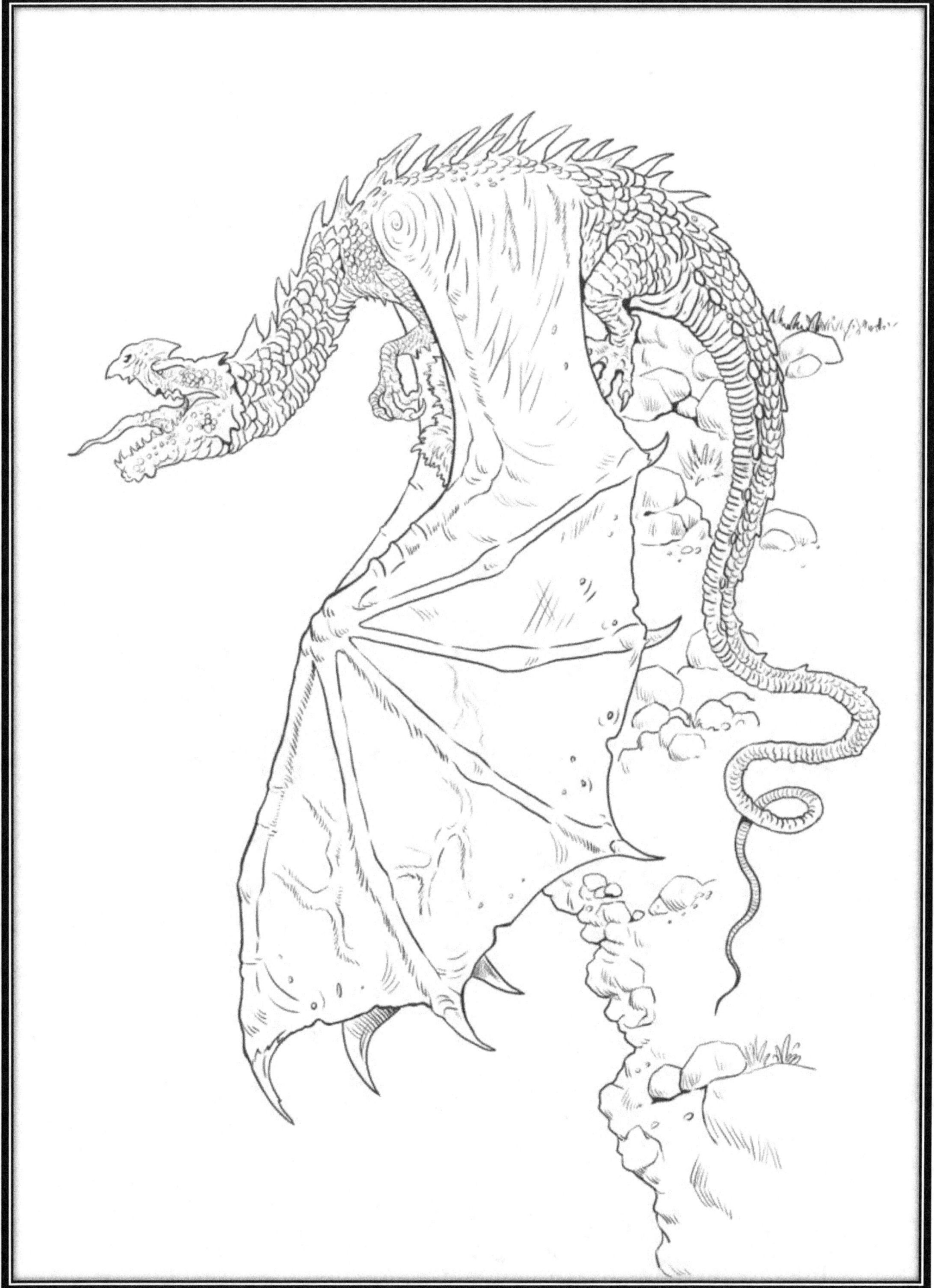

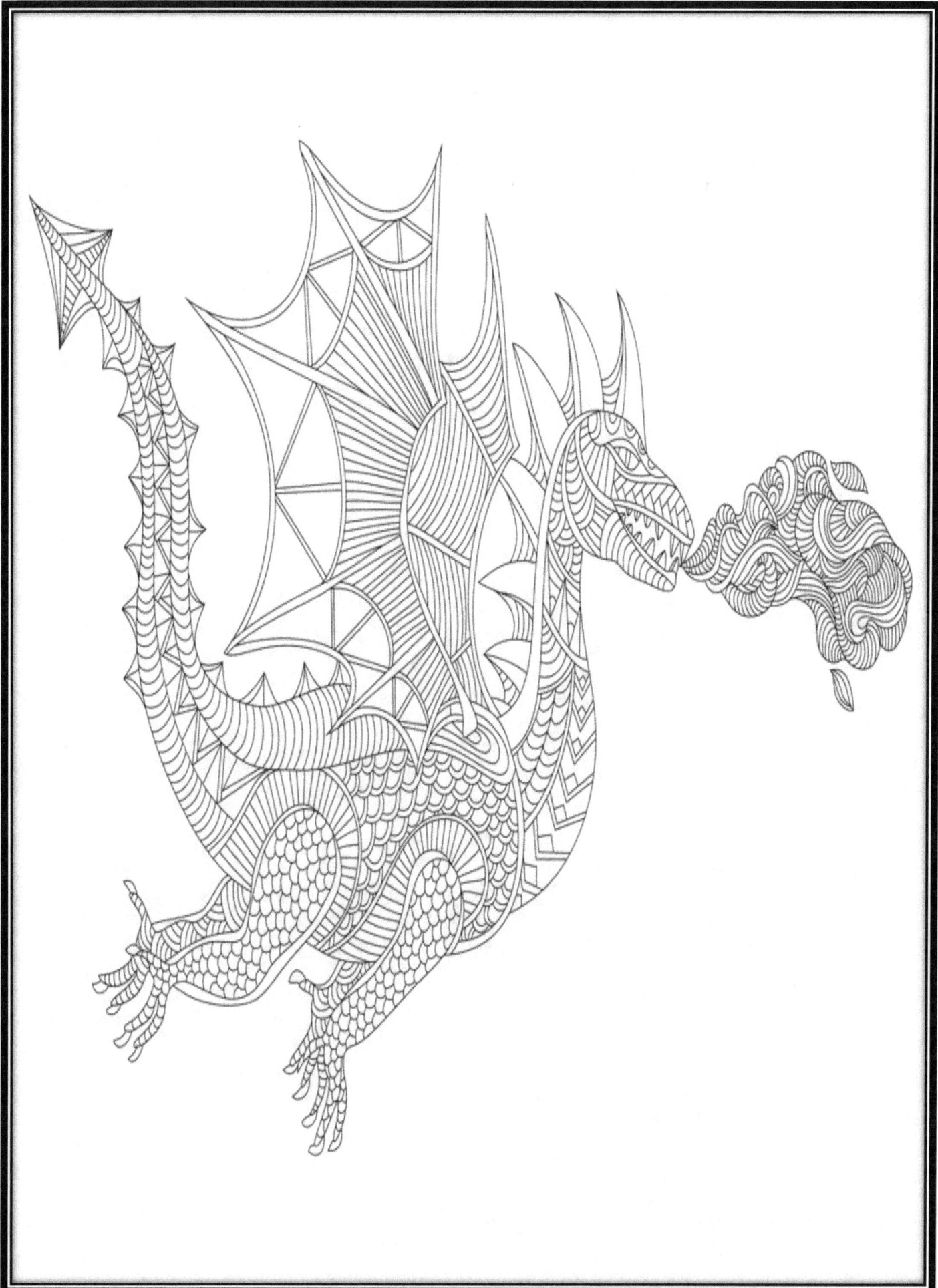

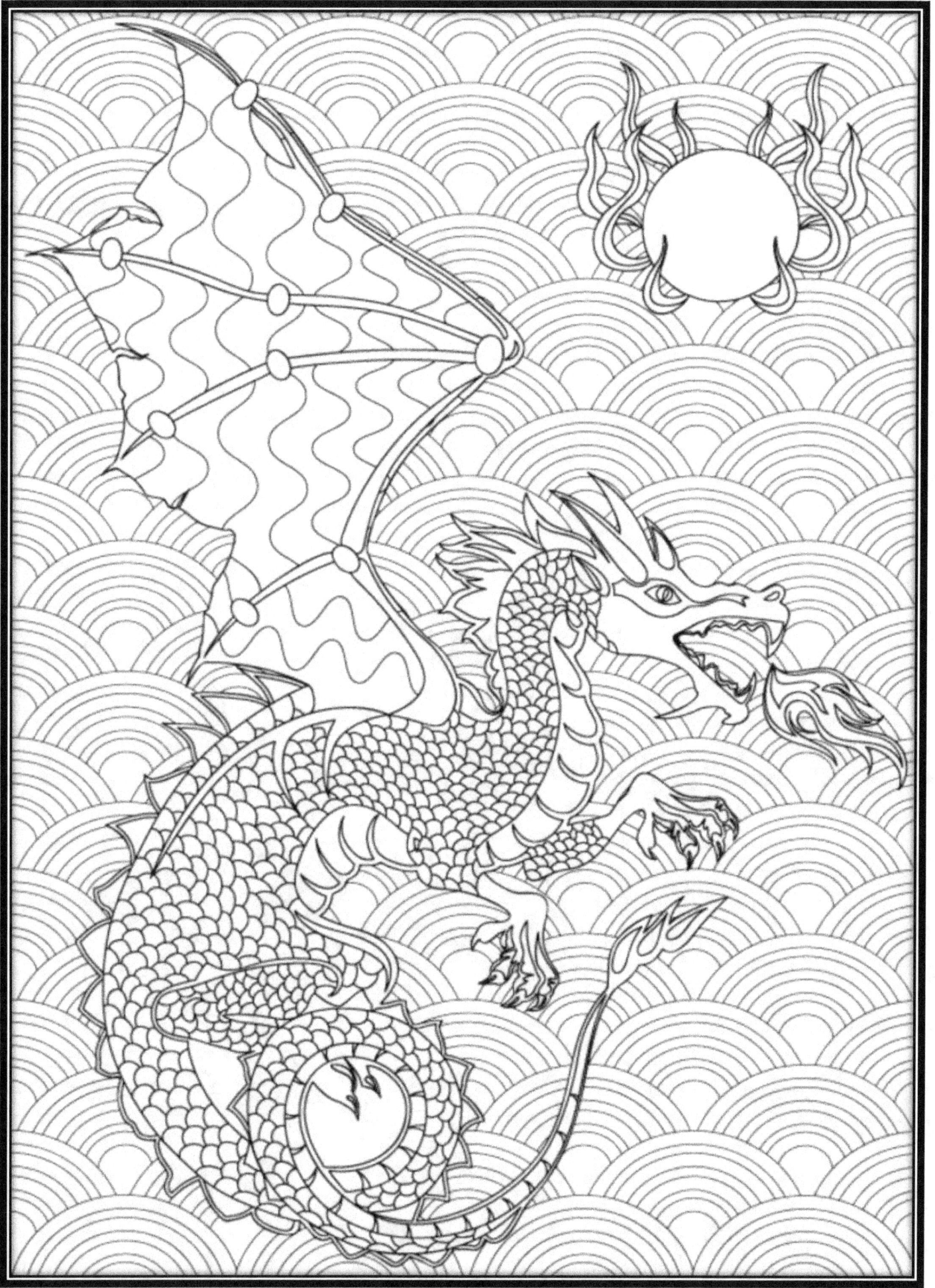

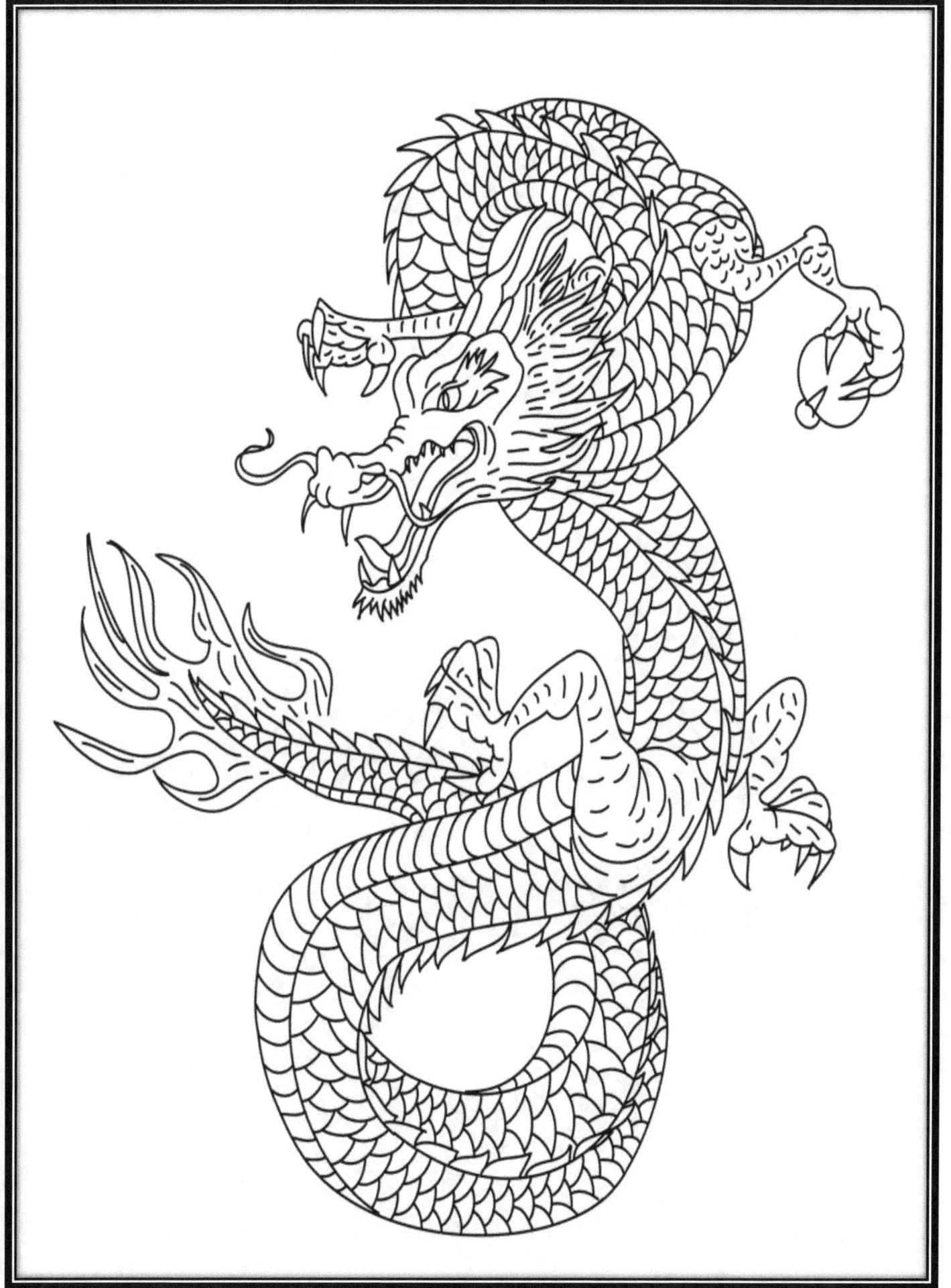

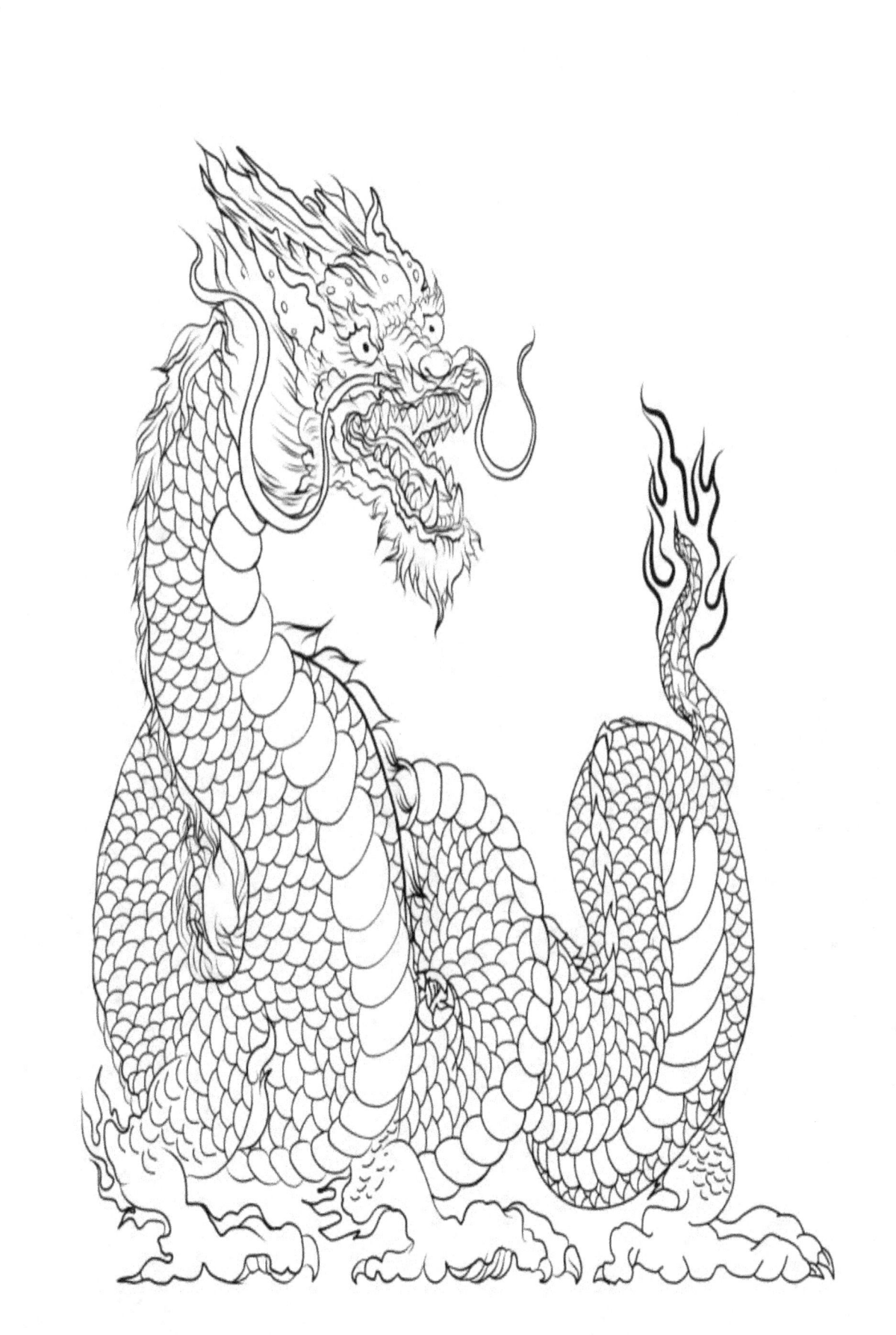

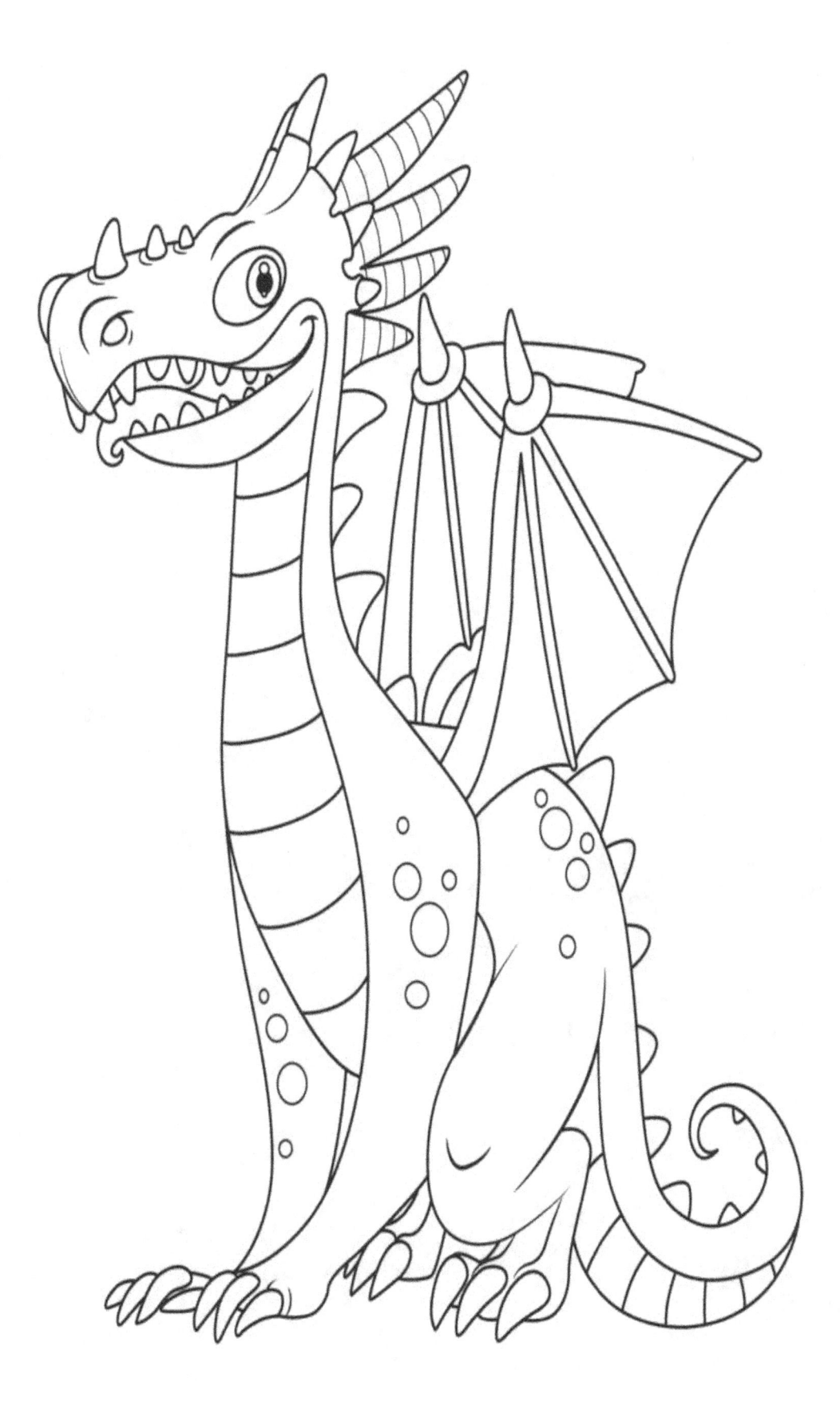

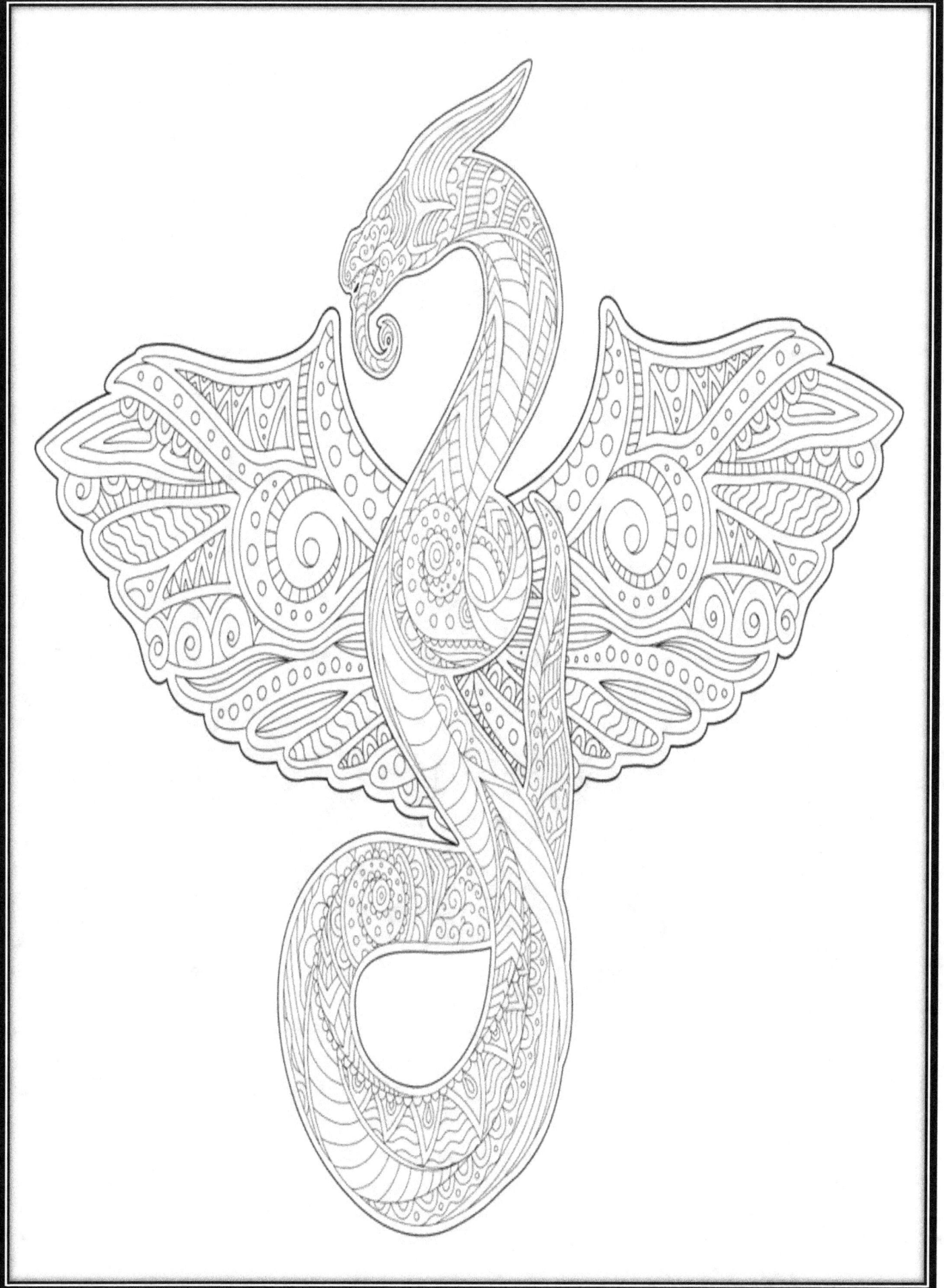

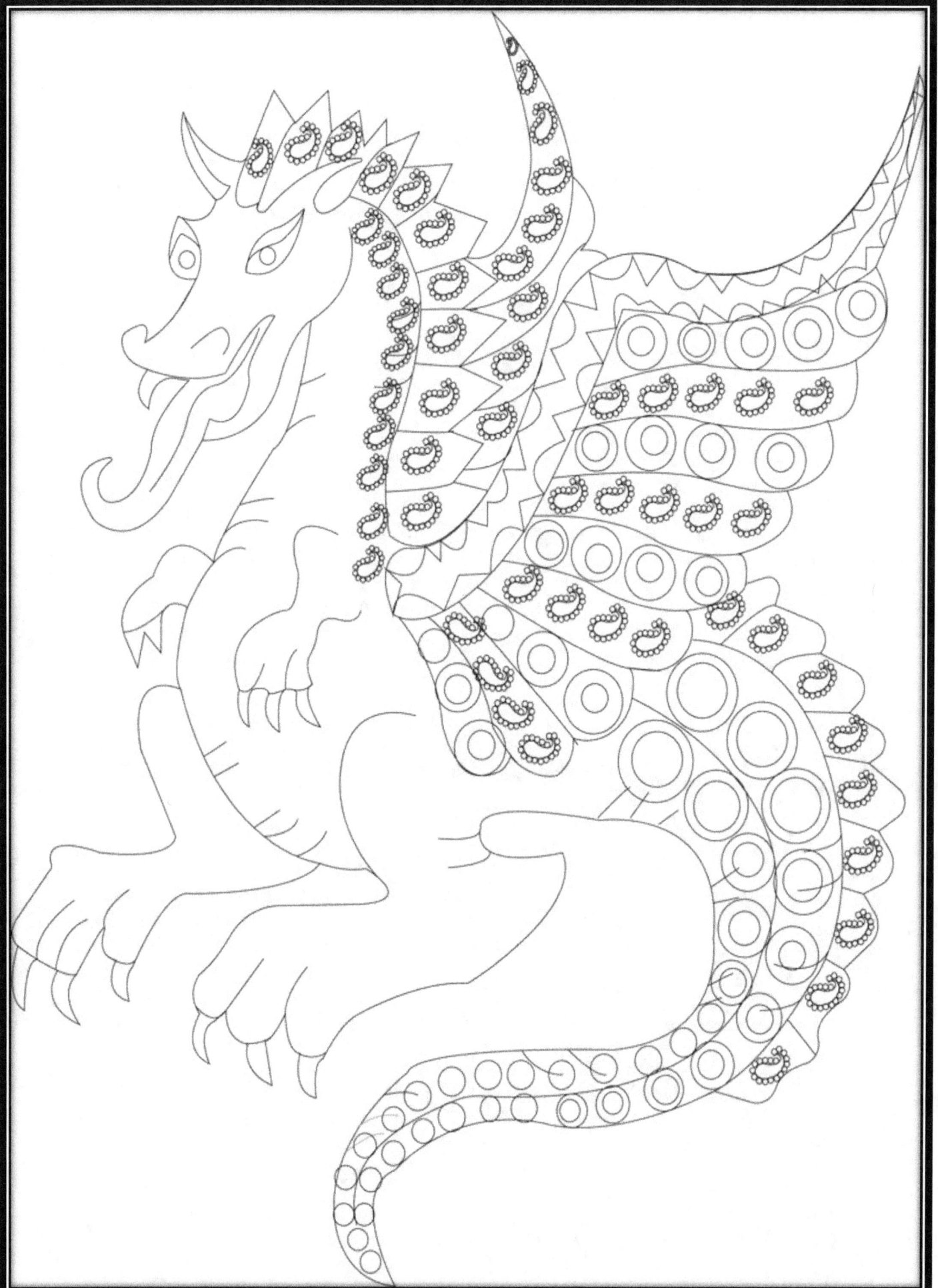

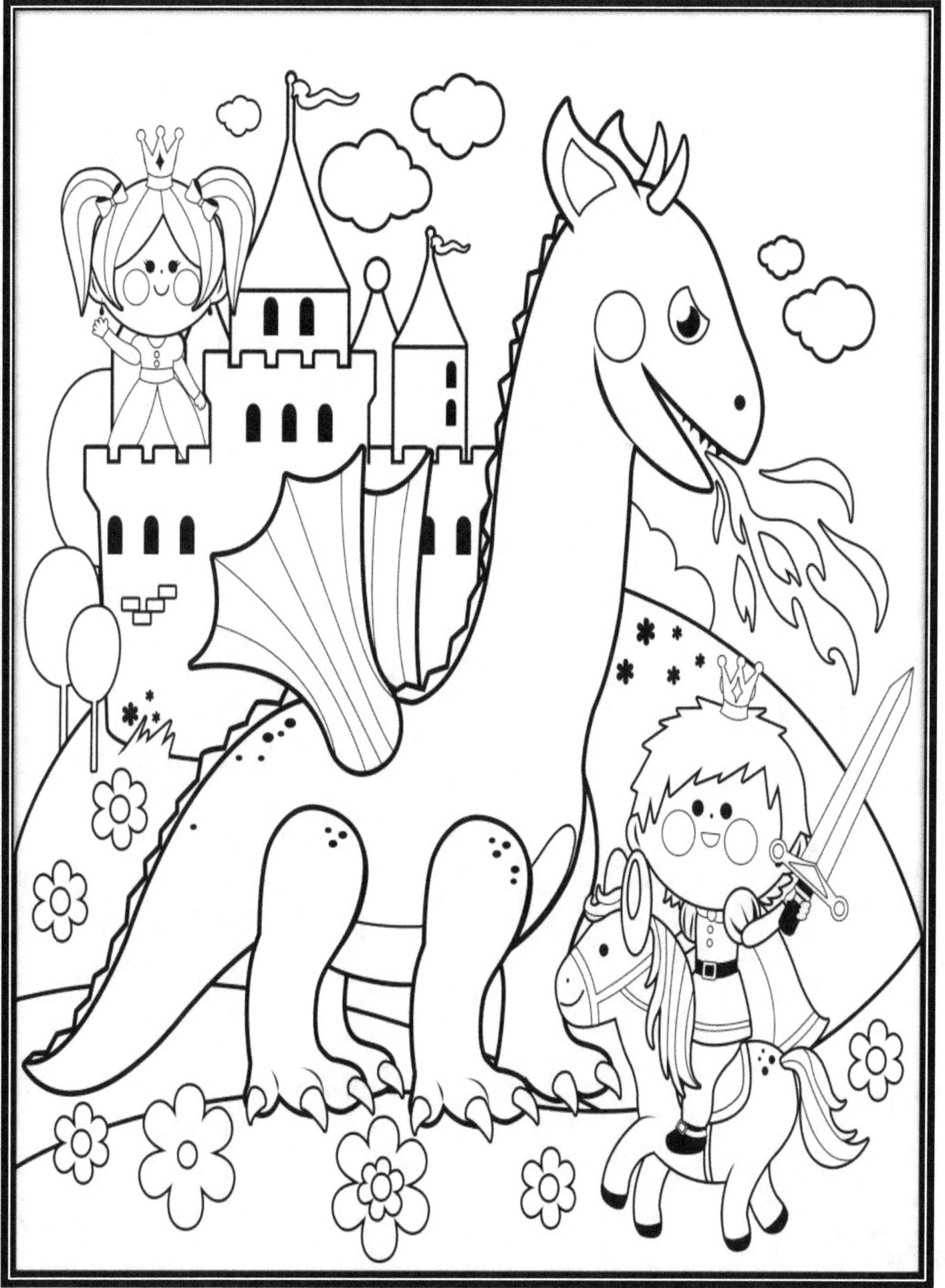

www.ingramcontent.com/pod-product-compliance
Lightning Source LLC
Chambersburg PA
CBHW081449220526
45466CB00008B/2561